S0-ABD-881

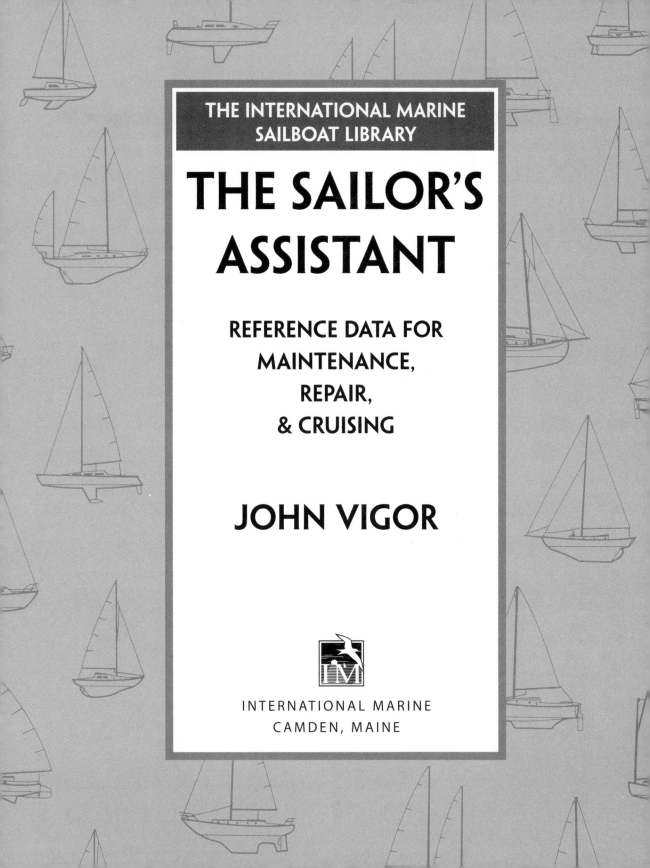

THE INTERNATIONAL MARINE SAILBOAT LIBRARY

THE SAILOR'S ASSISTANT

REFERENCE DATA FOR MAINTENANCE, REPAIR, & CRUISING

JOHN VIGOR

INTERNATIONAL MARINE
CAMDEN, MAINE

Contents

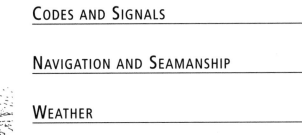

Preface

This book contains data needed sooner or later by anyone who cruises or races under sail. It's crammed with facts and figures relating to all aspects of designing, building, maintaining, repairing, and navigating a sailboat.

Active sailors and do-it-yourselfers constantly seek reference data: how much paint to buy, what size pilot holes to drill, what navigation lights to show, how much headroom to allow, how strong the rigging should be, what size propeller to order. Thousands of practical facts, figures, and timesaving tips are collated here in reader-friendly tables, lists, and charts catering to beginners, experienced hands, and amateur yacht designers.

No other similar work approaches it in scope. From the latest in high-tech electronics to the most humble cabin heater, you'll find it all here, right down to a list of sources of gear and information. The data is conveniently displayed for quick, intuitive access, and is backed up by a comprehensive index.

When might you need these facts and figures? When you're planning your dream boat. When you're buying a used boat, or taking delivery of a new boat. When you're comparing your boat with others. When you're on passage. When you're at anchor. When you're wondering where you'll find a replacement for your deteriorating plastic rubrail. And when you want to settle a bet.

This fingertip factfinder forms part of the International Marine Sailboat Library and complements the other volumes in the series.

JOHN VIGOR
Oak Harbor, WA
September 1996

 This symbol indicates a Rule of Thumb, or an estimation, tested by long experience, that brings results sufficiently accurate for the purpose.

 The Golden Rule symbol draws attention to a rule more precise and less flexible than a Rule of Thumb. It often applies to safety and should not be broken lightly.

Dinghies

INFLATABLE OR HARD DINGHY?

	Inflatable Dinghy	**Hard Dinghy**
PROS	Compact when deflated Fast with a small outboard Great load-carrying capacity Easy for swimmers to enter Doesn't damage your topsides	Better sea boat Easier to row and sail More durable Tows with less resistance More resistant to abrasion
CONS	Vulnerable to punctures Bouncy and wet under power Takes time to inflate/deflate	Less stable Heavier and bulkier Needs more stowage space

INFLATABLE DINGHY FACTS

Durability
- DuPont's Hypalon skin, recommended for tropics, is usually guaranteed for 10 years
- Polyvinyl chloride (PVC) material, excellent in temperate climates, is usually guaranteed for five years
- Inflatables subjected to abnormally rough use by liveaboard cruisers usually wear out in three or four years

Typical Weights and Dimensions
These measurements include integral floors but not removable floorboards. On some models, permanently installed floorboards can add about 50 percent to the hull weight.

Typical Measurements

LOA	Beam	Weight	Stowed Size	Persons
7'7" 2.3 m	4'1" 1.24 m	32 lb. 14.5 kg	33 × 17" (dia.) 84 × 43 cm (dia.)	3
8'6" 2.6 m	4'7" 1.4 m	49 lb. 22 kg	37 × 20 × 12" 94 × 51 × 30 cm	4
9'6" 2.9 m	4'7" 1.4 m	55 lb. 25 kg	37 × 20 × 14" 94 × 51 × 36 cm	4
10'0" 3.0 m	4'11" 1.5 m	68 lb. 31 kg	37 × 19 × 15" 94 × 48 × 38 cm	4
11'0" 3.4 m	4'11" 1.5 m	73 lb. 33 kg	39 × 23 × 17" 99 × 58 × 43 cm	4

Maximum Outboard Motor Power

(for inflatables with motor mount but no solid transom)

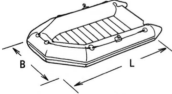

B =
Extreme beam

L = Overall length.

Length	Motor Power	
	Horsepower	Kilowatts
Less than 9' (2.7 m)	3.0	2.2
9 to 12' (2.7 to 3.6 m)	5.0	3.7
Over 12' (3.6 m)	7.5	5.6

Maximum Outboard Engine Power

(with solid transom)

The maximum outboard horsepower for inflatables with a transom may be calculated by multiplying length in feet (L) by beam in feet (B). If L × B is less than 35, maximum horsepower is 3 (2.2 kW). If the result is between 36 and 39, maximum horsepower is 5 (3.7 kW). If it is between 40 and 42, maximum horsepower is 7.5 (5.6 kW).

If L × B is between 43 and 80, for maximum horsepower multiply the figure obtained by 10, divide by 9, and subtract 40.

If L × B is more than 80, maximum horsepower is L × B divided by 2, plus 10. Examples are shown below, rounded up or down to the nearest appropriate engine size.

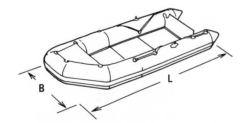

Length × Beam	Engine Power	
	Horsepower	Kilowatts
40 to 42	7.5	5.6
43	8.0	6.0
50	15.0	11.2
60	25.0	18.6
70	40.0	29.8
80	50.0	37.3
90	55.0	41.0

Note: Multiply horsepower by 0.7457 to convert to kilowatts.

Minimum Size

The smallest practical hard dinghy for two 160-pound (72-kg) people is a 7-foot (2-meter) pram weighing about 70 pounds (32 kg).

Safe Carrying Capacity

Refer to the "U.S. Coast Guard Maximum Capacities" label inside the transom of your dinghy for information about safe carrying capacity and maximum engine horsepower.

　　If there is no capacity label, the following formula approved by the U.S. Coast Guard Boating Education Branch determines the number of persons of average weight a boat under 20 feet (6 meters) will safely carry in calm weather. Weight for this purpose is usually taken to be 160 pounds (72 kg) per person.

$$\text{Number of people} = \frac{\text{overall length} \times \text{beam (in feet)}}{15}$$

OR

$$\text{Number of people} = \frac{\text{overall length} \times \text{beam (in meters)}}{1.4}$$

Example:

1. A 10-foot dinghy has a beam of 4.2 feet.
2. $10 \times 4.2 = 42 \div 15 = 2.8$ people.
3. Round up to 3 people.

Example:

1. A 3.6-meter dinghy has a beam of 1.28 m.
2. $3.6 \times 1.28 = 4.62 \div 1.4 = 3.3$ people.
3. Round down to 3 people.

Ideal Hard Tender

L. Francis Herreshoff's ideal tender would:

➤ row easily, light or loaded

➤ be light enough to be hoisted aboard easily

➤ be stiff enough to get into and out of easily

➤ be constructed strongly so she will not leak and will take some abuse

➤ tow steadily, always holding back on her painter and never yawing around

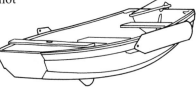

Saving Space   Some modern nesting designs stow compactly on the deck of a small yacht. The two halves fit one inside the other, and bolt or latch together before or after launching. For example, an 11-foot (3.3 m) nesting dinghy stows in a space only 5 feet 10 inches (1.78 m) long.

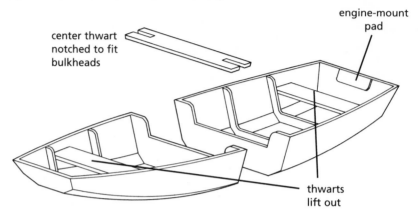

center thwart notched to fit bulkheads

engine-mount pad

thwarts lift out

Small folding dinghies made of plywood, canvas, and/or plastic may be bought or built from plans. They usually fold gunwale to gunwale. Typically, a 6-foot 8-inch (2.03-m) LOA folding boat with a beam of 4 feet 2 inches (1.27 m) will measure 7 feet 1 inch (2.16 m) × 1 foot 9 inches (533 mm) × 4.5 inches (114 mm) when folded.

Oar Length   (for average tenders)

This rule of thumb gives a "low gear" for easy pulling in a headwind or chop: The overall length of each oar should be roughly one and a half times the distance between oarlocks.

Example:

1. Beam between oarlocks = 48 inches (1.2 m).
2. Overall length of oar = 48 × 1.5 = 72 inches (1.8 m).

Oar Length   (for serious rowers in serious rowing boats)

1. Measure beam between oarlocks.
2. To find the inboard length of the oar, divide the beam measurement by 2, and add 2 inches (50 mm).
3. To find the total length of the oar, divide the inboard length by 7; then multiply by 25.

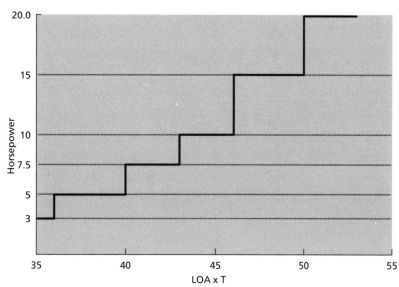

Example:

1. Beam between oarlocks = 38 inches (965 mm).

2. Inboard length of oar = (38 ÷ 2) + 2 = 21 inches (533 mm).

3. Total length of oar = (21 ÷ 7) × 25 = 75 inches (1.9 m).

Maximum Outboard Motor Power for Hard Dinghies For hard dinghies of less than 20 feet, multiply length overall (LOA) by the width of the transom (T), both in feet and to the nearest whole number. Check the result in the following table for maximum horsepower:

LOA × T	Horsepower
Up to 35	3.0
36 to 39	5.0
40 to 42	7.5
43 to 45	10.0
46 to 49	15.0
50 to 52	20.0

Example:

1. LOA = 10 feet.

2. T = 3 feet 10 inches.

3. LOA × T = 10 × 3.8 = 38.

4. Maximum outboard engine size = 5 hp.

Sculling a Dinghy   A sculling notch in the transom provides a way of getting home with one oar. Sculling over the stern is slower than rowing, and more tiring, but it is smoother and more powerful.

Because the oar blade is not exposed to the wind, sculling is especially useful over short distances in strong headwinds and choppy seas. The steady power of a sculling stroke obviates snatching when you are towing a heavier boat. Light, shallow dinghies need to be sculled with short, sharp strokes.

The usual size for a sculling notch is $1^7/8$ inches (47 mm) wide by $2^1/2$ inches (64 mm) deep. Typically, the notch is somewhat egg-shaped, widening slightly from top to bottom to discourage the oar loom from jumping out, and all edges are well rounded.

The notch may be offset slightly to one side or the other to allow an outboard motor to occupy the center of the transom. This offset is easily compensated for when you are sculling.

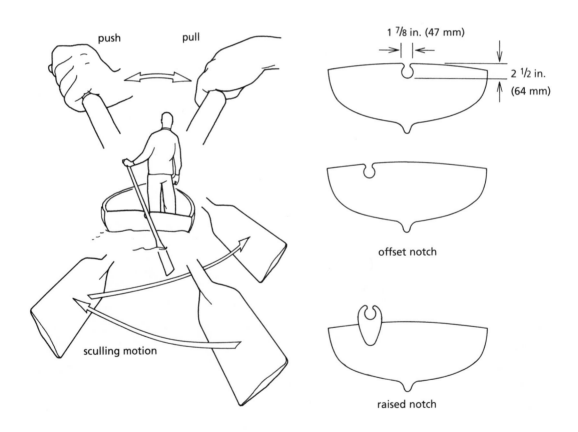

push   pull

sculling motion

1 $^7/8$ in. (47 mm)

2 $^1/2$ in. (64 mm)

offset notch

raised notch

SAIL AREAS FOR DINGHIES

These are average sail areas for nonplaning dinghies, used for cruising or day-sailing, between 8 feet (2.4 m) and 18 feet (5.5 m) long. Racing dinghies, obviously, will carry more sail.

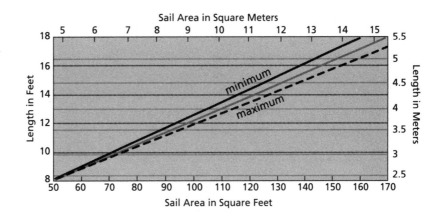

Planing Speed of Hard Dinghies

The approximate speed in knots at which most planing dinghies start to plane may be calculated as follows:

Find the square root of the waterline length in feet and multiply by 2.2.

Example:

$$\sqrt{10} = 3.162$$
$$3.162 \times 2.2 = 6.9564$$
$$= 7.$$

A 10-foot-waterline dinghy will start to plane at just under 7 knots.

Deck Gear

**Common Anchor
Types and Uses**

Anchor Type		Trade Name	Bottom Type			
			Weeds/Grass	Rock	Sand	Mud
Plow, non-pivoting		Delta	adequate	poor	good	poor
Plow, pivoting		CQR	adequate	adequate	good	adequate
Winged scoop		Bruce	poor	adequate	good	adequate
Lightweight, pivoting fluke		Danforth	poor	poor	good	adequate
		Fortress	poor	poor	good	adequate
		Guardian	poor	poor	adequate	poor
		Performance	poor	poor	good	adequate
Fisherman, traditional		Herreshoff	good	good	adequate	poor
		Luke	good	good	adequate	poor

**Anchor and Rode
Sizes Relative
to Boat Length**
These sizes are conservative minimums for plow-type anchors on boats of medium displacement under normal conditions. Boats with heavier displacement, or greater windage than normal, or boats experiencing rougher than normal conditions, will need heavier ground tackle.

Pivoting-fluke anchors (Danforth type) give greater holding power for much less weight, provided they can dig into sand or mud.

Fisherman-type anchors should weigh about 2 pounds per foot of water-line length (3 kg per meter of waterline length).

In all cases, storm anchors should be two sizes bigger.

The chain part of the rode should be at least as long as the boat. Boats over 25 feet (8 m) in length may benefit from an all-chain rode.

Three-strand nylon, which has the ability to stretch and absorb shock loading, is recommended for the rope part of the rode.

Boat Length	Plow Anchor Weight	Rope Diameter	Chain Diameter
Up to 21 ft.	11 lb.	7/16 in.	3/16 in.
Up to 6.4 m	5 kg	11 mm	5 mm
22–25 ft.	22 lb.	1/2 in.	1/4 in.
6.7–7.5 m	10 kg	13 mm	6 mm
26–30 ft.	25 lb.	9/16 in.	1/4 in.
8.0–9.0 m	11 kg	14 mm	6 mm
31–40 ft.	35 lb.	9/16 in.	5/16 in.
9.4–12.0 m	16 kg	14 mm	8 mm
41–45 ft.	44 lb.	5/8 in.	3/8 in.
12–14.0 m	20 kg	16 mm	10 mm
46–50 ft.	55 lb.	3/4 in.	3/8 in.
14–15.0 m	25 kg	19 mm	10 mm

Length of Anchor Rode

How long should your anchor rode (rope plus chain) be? The rule of thumb is a minimum of 1 fathom (6 feet) for every foot of the boat's overall length. In metric terms, that is 6 meters of rode for every meter of boat length.

Example:

1. Boat is 34 feet (10.4 m) long.

2. Minimum anchor rode required = 34 × 6 = 204 feet (62.4 meters).

Anchor Rode Stowage Space

The size of a self-stowing chain locker may be estimated thus:

Volume in cubic feet = (fathoms chain × diameter in inches^2) × 0.85

To find the volume needed for every 10 fathoms (60 feet) or 18 meters of chain, refer to the table that follows on page 14.

Chain Stowage Space

Diameter of chain		Cubic feet	Cubic meters
3/16 in.	5 mm	0.30	0.008
1/4 in.	6.5 mm	0.53	0.015
5/16 in.	8 mm	0.83	0.023
3/8 in.	10 mm	1.20	0.034

Note: Rope typically requires more locker space than chain of equal length and equivalent strength because it does not compact itself as chain does to take advantage of all the space available. The amount of extra space depends on the rope's material and its method of construction, both of which affect its flexibility and therefore its natural tendency to fake down tightly, but the three-stranded nylon rope usually used for anchoring will normally require at least 25 percent more locker room if it is self-stowing.

Chain Strength and Weight

Proof-coil chain is made from low-carbon steel. It has relatively long links. Breaking strength is three and a half to four times the working load limit.

BBB chain is made from the same material as proof-coil, but has shorter links and works better in windlasses. Breaking strength is three and a half to four times the working load limit.

High-test chain has a higher carbon content and is stronger than proof-coil and BBB chain. It is therefore lighter for the same strength but rusts faster. High-test chain can be one size smaller than proof coil or BBB. Breaking strength is about three times the working load limit.

All three types are supplied ready galvanized and all three are suitable for anchor chain. BBB is most popular on cruising boats with windlasses and all-chain rodes. Proof-coil is usually used in conjunction with nylon rope on boats without windlasses, and the lighter high-test chain is used extensively on performance cruisers.

proof coil

BBB chain

high-test chain

BBB Chain

Diameter		Working Load		Weight	
Inches	mm	Pounds	kg	Pounds/Foot	kg/m
3/16	5	800	363	0.43	0.64
1/4	6.5	1,325	601	0.76	1.13
5/16	8	1,950	884	1.13	1.68
3/8	10	2,750	1,247	1.64	2.44
7/16	11	3,625	1,644	2.22	3.30
1/2	13	4,750	2,155	2.85	4.24
9/16	14	5,875	2,665	3.55	5.28
5/8	16	7,250	3,288	4.25	6.32
3/4	19	10,250	4,649	6.15	9.15

These formulas give a rough estimate of the maximum working load for galvanized steel shackles and hooks. These loads, based on industrial safety standards, are about 11 to 12 percent of the breaking loads. (For less rigorous, more occasional use on non-commercial boats, working loads of 25 percent to $33^{1}/_{3}$ percent are often recommended by retailers.)

shackle

D = the pin diameter in inches, and results are in tons.
Multiply tons by 1,016 to convert to kilograms.

Straight shackle	$3 \times D^2$
Bow shackle	$2.5 \times D^2$
Ring bolt	$2 \times D^2$
Eyebolt	$5 \times D^2$
Hook	$0.67 \times D^2$ when D is the diameter in inches at the base, where the main shank enters the throat.

eyebolt

hook

For working loads in kilograms, measure the diameter in millimeters, apply the formulas above, and multiply the result by 1.58.

Example:

1. A bow shackle on an anchor rode has a diameter (D) of $^3/_8$ inch.

2. Safe working load (SWL) = $2.5 \times (^3/_8)^2$ = 0.35 tons.

3. SWL = $0.35 \times 2{,}240$ = 784 pounds (356 kg).

BLOCKS, SHEAVES, AND TACKLES

Sheave Diameters for Wire and Rope

Ideally, wire rope sheaves should have a diameter of not less than 40 times the wire diameter for long life and easy rendering. In actual use, such ideal proportions are rarely achieved. In extremis, and for short periods, the ideal sheave diameter may be halved, but the wire's strength will be severely compromised and its life shortened.

Similarly, fiber rope needs a sheave diameter of not less than eight times the rope diameter if undue stress and premature wear are to be avoided. But, once again, smaller sheaves and more frequent replacement of lines are choices often forced upon us.

The table on page 16 shows the recommended diameter of that part of the sheave upon which the rope bears.

Line Diameter		Wire Sheave Diameter		Rope Sheave Diameter	
Inches	mm	Inches	mm	Inches	mm
1/8	3	5	127	1	25
5/32	4	6 1/4	160	1 1/4	32
3/16	5	7 1/2	190	1 1/2	38
7/32	5.5	8 3/4	225	1 3/4	45
1/4	6.4	10	250	2	50
5/16	8	12 1/2	320	2 1/2	65
3/8	9	15	380	3	75
7/16	11	—	—	3 1/2	90
1/2	12.7	—	—	4	100
5/8	15.8	—	—	5	130
3/4	19	—	—	6	150
7/8	22	—	—	7	180
1	25			8	200

Block and Tackle Mechanical Advantage

To calculate the mechanical advantage of a block and tackle, first separate the moving blocks from the stationary blocks.

Then count the number of parts in the moving block or blocks. The number of parts equals the mechanical advantage.

A *part*, in this instance, means a line where it enters, or where it leaves, the block. (One line entering a block, rounding a sheave and then exiting again counts as two parts.) A line attached to the shell or becket of a moving block is a part, but a line attached to the load is not.

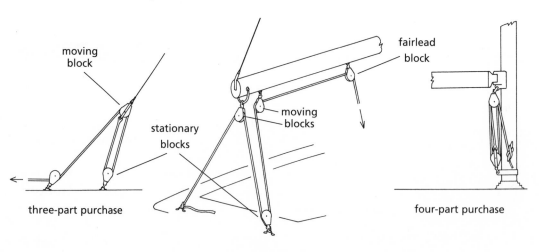

three-part purchase

four-part purchase

four-part purchase

Loads on Turning Blocks

The load on a block varies with the turning angle, that is the angle formed at the sheave by the line where it enters and where it leaves the block.

A line that makes a 180-degree turn around a sheave, such as a main halyard block, will exert a force on the sheave of double the line load. Lesser turns will experience less block loading. For example, a turn of 90 degrees effects a block loading of 141 percent of the line load.

Any block subjected to acute turning angles, such as a genoa or spinnaker sheet turning block, or a halyard block, must be strong enough to bear the increased loading. Calculate turning block loads as follows:

Sheave load = line load × the turning angle factor.

Example:

1. A genoa lead block turns the sheet through 30 degrees.

2. The load on the genoa sheet is 250 pounds (110 kg).

3. The load on the block is 250 pounds (110 kg) × 30° turning angle factor
= 250 (110) × 0.518 = 129.5 pounds (56.9 kg).

Angle	Turning Factor
0°	0
30°	0.518
45°	0.767
60°	1.00
90°	1.414
120°	1.732
135°	1.846
150°	1.931
180°	2.0

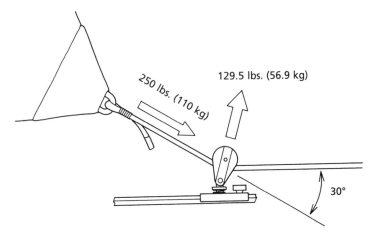

CLEAT TYPES AND USES

Cam Cleats

Advantages:
➤ Instant control
➤ No slippage
➤ Lightweight
➤ Easy to release

Disadvantages:
➤ Teeth tend to wear smooth and lose grip
➤ May abrade rope
➤ Different sizes needed for different lines
➤ Line release is uncontrolled

Used for: All control lines loaded to a maximum of about 500 pounds.

Clam Cleats

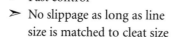

Advantages:

➣ Fast control
➣ No slippage as long as line size is matched to cleat size
➣ No moving parts

Disadvantages:

➣ May be difficult to release under extreme load
➣ Different sizes needed for various-sized ropes

Used for: Control lines, especially on custom-made fittings, from dinghies through ocean racers.

Horned Cleats

Advantages:

➣ Sturdiest and simplest
➣ Large sizes fit all lines
➣ Lines can be finely controlled by surging on release
➣ Accept up to four fasteners, instead of two
➣ No moving parts
➣ Can be made from wood, plastic, or metal

Disadvantages:

➣ More prone to snag moving lines
➣ Slower to make fast and release

Used for: All purposes—sheets, halyards, mooring lines, dinghy painters, anchor rodes, and so on, down to flag halyards.

 Whenever possible, a horned cleat should be fastened at an angle of about 15 degrees to the direction of the line's pull. Its length should be at least 12 times, and preferably 16 times, the diameter of the rope used with it.

Jam Cleats

Advantages:

➣ Quicker in use than horned cleats, which they most closely resemble
➣ Significantly faster to release

Disadvantages:

➣ Rope size must be compatible for the best results
➣ May not release easily, or at all, if line is shock-loaded
➣ Line not easily controllable after release, except that it may be jammed again

Used for: Frequently handled sheets and other control lines, mostly on racing sailboats.

Minimum Sizes for Nylon Dock Lines

Diameter: 1/8 inch (3 mm) for every 9 feet (2.7 m) overall boat length.

Length: Bow and stern lines, two-thirds of overall boat length. Spring lines, one and a quarter times as long as the boat.

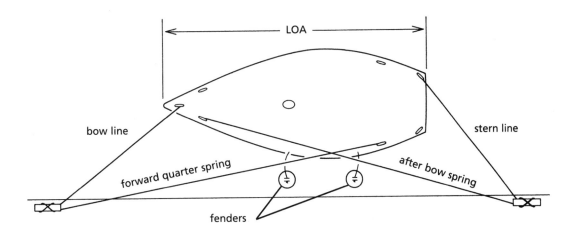

DECK GEAR

Fender Sizes

The diameter of fenders should be about 1 inch for every 5 feet of boat length, or 16 mm for every 1 meter.

HATCH SIZES

Absolute minimum size for a person to get through:
22 inches × 22 inches (560 mm × 560 mm)

Normal size for an access hatch:
24 inches × 24 inches (610 mm × 610 mm)

Minimum size to pass a sail through:
Racing boats:
Sail area ÷ 160 = hatch area
(in square feet or square meters)

Cruising boats:
Sail area ÷ 200 = hatch area
(in square feet or square meters)

LIFELINE SIZES

Most boats of 25 feet (8 m) or less use $\frac{1}{8}$-inch (3 mm) stainless steel wire for lifelines. Larger boats use $\frac{3}{16}$-inch (5 mm) stainless wire. Plastic-covered wire is vulnerable to corrosion if salt water penetrates the plastic, and the corrosion may not be visible. Bare wire, 1×19 stainless steel, grade 18-8, is preferred by most cruisers.

The height of the upper lifelines should never be less than 30 inches (760 mm) above deck. Anything lower is of questionable value and may even be worse than no lifelines at all. Unusually low lifelines can actually help tip a crewmember overboard. Crews on boats without any lifelines at all tend to take more precautions when moving around on deck.

VENTILATORS—COMPARATIVE EFFICIENCY

The natural flow of air inside most sailboats that have forehatches hinged along the forward edge, is from aft forward, particularly if a main companionway dodger is fitted. It hardly seems to matter which way the wind is blowing.

Fans or passive ventilators should be placed to take advantage of this natural circulation.

Don't forget that a 4-inch (100 mm) diameter vent handles almost twice as much air as a 3-inch (75 mm) vent. The latter is most often found on sailboats, where large cowls are likely to be snagged by running rigging, but the former should really be regarded as the minimum size for boats up to 40 feet (12 meters) long.

All ventilators, including those fitted with Dorade-type water traps, should be capable of being sealed from down below.

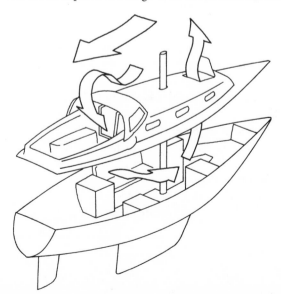

Manufacturers classify their winches according to the leverage they produce, and call it a power ratio. For example, a No. 16 winch will pull about 160 pounds (or kilograms) for every 10 pounds (10 kg) of force you put into turning the handle. This table lists the power ratios of commonly available winches. It suggests ranges for boats of average displacement and sail area. Heavy-displacement yachts should use winches a size bigger.

Application	Overall Boat Length				
	20–25 Ft. 6–8 m	25–30 Ft. 8–9 m	30–35 Ft. 9–10 m	35–40 Ft. 10–12 m	40–50 Ft. 12–14 m
Foreguy	—	—	6–8	16	30
Jib halyard	8	16	24–30	40–44	46
Jib, genoa sheet	8	24	30–46	48	54
Main halyard	6	8	16–24	30–40	40–46
Mainsheet	—	6	8–16	24–30	40–44
Reefing lines	—	6	8–16	16–24	30–40
Runners	6	8	16–30	30–40	40–46
Spinnaker halyard	6	8	16–24	30–40	44–46
Spinnaker sheet	6	16	16–30	40–44	46–54
Topping lift	—	—	6–8	8–16	30

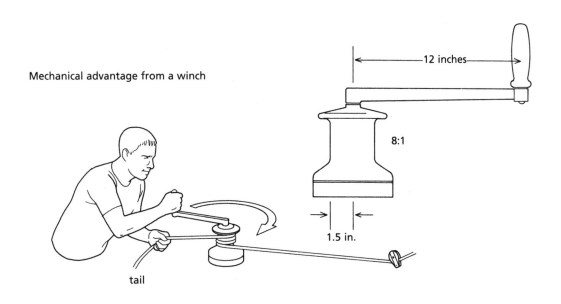

Mechanical advantage from a winch

12 inches

8:1

1.5 in.

tail

Electrical Systems

Ohm's Law Every electrical circuit on a boat is governed by the basic physical law discovered by Georg Simon Ohm. It defines the relationship between voltage, current, and resistance. Ohm's Law states that

$$I = E \div R, \quad \text{OR} \quad \text{amps} = \text{volts} \div \text{ohms};$$
$$R = E \div I, \quad \text{OR} \quad \text{ohms} = \text{volts} \div \text{amps};$$
$$E = I \times R, \quad \text{OR} \quad \text{volts} = \text{amps} \times \text{ohms}.$$

where I = amps, E = volts, and R = ohms.

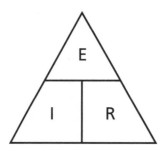

In the triangle above, cover with a finger the unit you want to find. The formula is given by the two visible units.

In Simple Terms . . .
- Amps measure the rate of current flow.
- Ohms measure a circuit's resistance to the flow of electricity.
- Volts indicate the electric "pressure" available to force the current through a resistance.
- Watts measure electrical power.
- Watts = amps × volts.
- Watt-hours represent the total number of watts used in one hour.
- Amp-hours represent the total number of amps used in one hour.

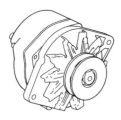

Engine-driven alternators are usually geared up to run faster than the engine. This is achieved by making the pulley wheel on the alternator smaller in diameter than the pulley on the engine. Most alternators must spin at a minimum of 5,000 rpm for maximum output, and can run at 10,000 rpm without damage.

Output rises rapidly with increased rpm, and then usually levels off between 5,000 and 6,000 rpm. Output also decreases with a rise in temperature, so that at 80°F (26°C) an alternator will usually generate 25 percent more power than it will at 200°F (94°C). Most engine-driven alternators run at about 130°F (55°C).

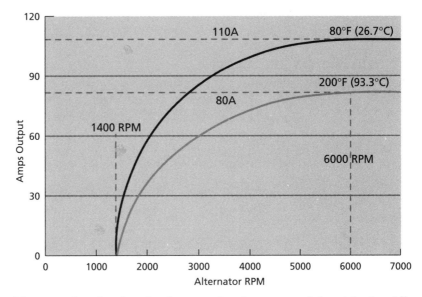

ELECTRICAL SYSTEMS

Power Needed to Drive an Alternator

It's easy to imagine that the alternator is a free source of electricity, just idly spinning away as the engine runs. But in fact it absorbs power from the engine in relation to the number of kilowatts it produces.

 The horsepower drain on the engine is twice the number of kilowatts produced.

Example:

1. A 100-amp alternator charges a 12-volt battery at 13.8 volts.
2. Watts (volts × amps) produced by alternator = 13.8 × 100 = 1,380.
3. Kilowatts produced = 1,380 ÷ 1,000 = 1.38.
4. Horsepower absorbed from engine = 1.38 × 2 = 2.76.

Correct Size of Alternator

A modern multistage regulator allows faster charging from a larger alternator. Used with a "smart" regulator, the alternator's rating in amps should equal 25 to 40 percent of the battery bank's capacity in amp-hours.

Example:

1. The storage capacity of a battery bank is 200 amp-hours.

2. The output amperage of the charging alternator should be between 25 and 40 percent of 200.

3. $0.25 \times 200 = 50; 0.40 \times 200 = 80$.

4. Required alternator charging power $= 50$ to 80 amps.

 Lacking a "smart" regulator, you should limit the charging rate in amps to 10 percent of the battery's capacity in amp-hours. Faster charging without proper regulation will greatly shorten battery life.

Correct Size of Battery Charger

A battery charger working off a 110-volt AC supply should have an output in amps of about 10 percent of your total battery amp-hours. If the charger also supplies DC current to onboard lights, appliances, or instruments, that load must be calculated and added to the 10 percent.

Example:

1. Battery bank = 2×100 amp-hour batteries = 200 amp-hours of capacity.

2. Required charger output is 10 percent of 200 = 20 amps.

3. Maximum extra DC current load (intermittent) = cabin lights, 48 watts; bilge pump, 48 watts; tape deck, 15 watts = 111 watts total = 9.25 amps at 12 volts. Round up to 10 amps.

4. Required charger output $= 20 + 10 = 30$ amps.

COMPARATIVE EFFICIENCY OF OTHER GENERATORS

These are rough comparisons, taken from manufacturers' brochures, of the electrical output of alternators—one driven by a propeller dragged through the water behind a boat, the other by a wind propeller—and solar panels.

wind
generator

Source	Output	Operating Hours	Total Amp-Hours
Water	5.25 amps at 5 knots	12	63
Wind	7.0 amps (15-mph wind)	12	84
Solar	2.64 amps (two 35-watt panels, average day)	12	32

Output of Solar Panels

The brighter the sun and the longer it shines, the more electricity a solar panel will generate. Its efficiency also depends on the angle at which the sun's rays strike the panel—it performs best when the rays are perpendicular.

Panel generates most electricity when it is angled at 90° to the sun. This graph shows approximate efficiency at other angles.

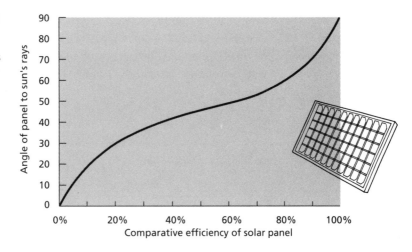

The three main types of solar panels are monocrystalline, polycrystalline, and thin-film panels. Monocrystalline panels, the most efficient, are also the most expensive. They and the polycrystalline panels are almost rigid. Thin-film panels are flexible, but far less efficient than the other two types.

 A rigid solar panel will generate, in amp-hours (*Ah*), about 25 percent of its rated wattage (*W*) each day. That is:

$$Ah \text{ generated per 12 hours } = W \times 0.25.$$

Example:

1. A rigid panel is rated at 35 watts.
2. Approximate daily output in amp-hours $= 35 \times 0.25 = 8.75$.

If the panel is adjusted all day long to face the sun squarely, its output may be double that stated in the above rule of thumb.

STORING ELECTRICITY

Automobile batteries are not recommended for use in auxiliary sailboats other than to start the engine. Car battery manufacturers assume that the battery will be charged fully immediately after the drain of starting the engine, but sailboat house batteries need to satisfy lesser current demands for much longer periods, and their design must allow them to discharge more deeply before being recharged. Automotive starting batteries are not designed for repeated deep discharge and will fail if subjected to it.

Marine deep-cycle batteries cost up to 20 percent more than car batteries of the same amp-hour capacity, but are longer-lived and more tolerant of abuse.

Calculating Your Battery Needs

Batteries come in various sizes, rated in amp-hours. An amp-hour is the amount of electricity used by an appliance drawing 1 amp for 1 hour.

Calculate your average daily amp-hour requirements by listing the electrical items you use during an average day and the length of time they're in use. Such items are usually rated in watts, so it is convenient to calculate in watts and then convert the total into amps at the end.

Average Daily Watt-Hour Totals

Appliance	Watts Consumed	Hours of Use	Daily Watt-Hours
Anchor light	10	10	100.0
Bilge pump	48	0.2	9.6
Cabin fan	12	6	72.0
Cabin lights	48	5	240.0
Instruments	12	3	36.0
Inverter	60	4.3	258.0
AM/FM radio	2	4	8.0
Starter motor	2,400	0.006	14.4
SSB radio (on standby)	12	3	36.0
SSB radio (transmit)	240	0.3	72.0
Tape deck	15	4	60.0
VHF (receive)	6	12	72.0
VHF (transmit)	60	0.2	12.0
Water pump	48	0.25	12.0
Windlass	240	0.16	38.4
Daily watt-hour total:			1,040.4

Divide total watt-hours by the number of volts in the circuit to get amp-hours, which you can more easily relate to your battery storage capacity.

Thus, for a 12-volt system, 1,040.4 watt-hours ÷ 12 = 86.7 amp-hours. Call this 90 amp-hours.

 Only 40 percent of your total battery capacity is available for normal use.

So the battery capacity necessary to sustain 90 amp-hours a day is 225 amp-hours (40 percent of 225 = 90). If you were generous in your estimates and determined to save more energy in future, you could probably settle for two batteries rated at 100 amp-hours each.

Each one, in theory, could supply 5 amps for 20 hours at 80°F (27°C), or 20 amps for five hours, and so on. But it's difficult to top up the last 10 percent of a battery's capacity during ordinary recharging, and it isn't good for the battery's life (even a deep-cycle battery's) to let it drop below 50 percent of capacity before recharging—hence the 40 percent rule.

If you have no way of ascertaining the wattage or amperage of an appliance on your boat, the following table will give a rough idea of average loads, in watts, on a 12-volt DC system.

Average Wattage Loads

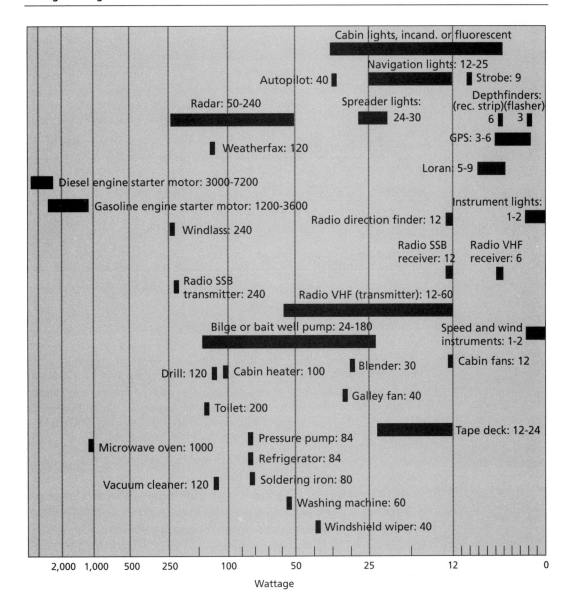

Condition of Lead-Acid Batteries

Because the specific gravity (SG), or density, of a cell's electrolyte varies with its state of charge, a hydrometer reading will give a good indication of the battery's condition. Most manufacturers rate the SG of a fully charged cell at 1.260 at 77°F with the electrolyte just covering the top of the plates.

Apply these corrections for temperature and electrolyte level:

Add one gravity point (0.001) for each 3° above 77°F;
OR
Subtract one gravity point for each 3° below 77°F.

Add 15 points (0.015) for each half-inch electrolyte level is above normal;
OR
Subtract 15 points for each half-inch electrolyte level is below normal.

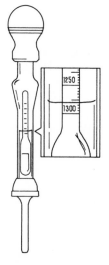

Hydrometer Reading by Temperature

Battery Condition	50°F 10°C	60°F 16°C	70°F 21°C	80°F 27°C	90°F 32°C	100°F 38°C	110°F 43°C
Fully charged	1.288	1.284	1.280	1.276	1.272	1.268	1.264
Half-charged	1.208	1.204	1.200	1.196	1.192	1.188	1.184
Fully discharged	1.118	1.114	1.110	1.106	1.102	1.098	1.094

Amp-Hour Ratings

The manufacturer's amp-hour rating indicates the total amount of energy a battery will deliver at a constant rate of discharge over a period of 20 hours, before voltage reaches 10.5, at which stage it is dead for all practical purposes.

This means a 100 amp-hour battery can run a constant 5-amp load for 20 hours. Similarly, a 200-amp-hour battery can run a constant 10-amp load for 20 hours.

But if a 100-amp-hour battery is discharged at a rate greater than 5 amps, it will deliver fewer amp-hours than advertised. In other words, if it is discharged at, say, 10 amps, instead of 5 amps, it will be dead before 10 hours is up.

Conversely, if it is discharged at a rate of less than 5 amps, it will produce a few more amp-hours than shown on the manufacturer's rating. That principle applies to most lead-acid batteries—the faster the discharge rate, the fewer amp-hours delivered.

Cranking Ratings   The engine-starting ability of a battery is often marked on the casing by the manufacturer in cold cranking amps (CCA) or marine cranking amps (MCA).

CCA defines the useful number of amps delivered for 30 seconds at 0°F (–18°C). The larger the figure, the bigger the engine the battery will crank.

MCA is the same thing, but measured at 32°F (0°C). Batteries gain efficiency with warmth, so MCA figures would normally be about 20 percent greater than CCA figures for the same battery.

 For diesel engines, allow 2 cold cranking amps (CCAs) per cubic inch of piston displacement. For gas engines, allow 1 CCA per cubic inch.

Effect of Temperature on Battery Power

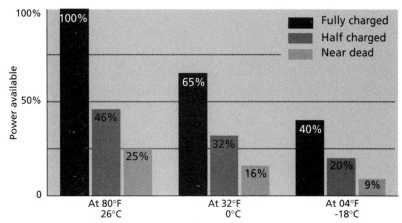

Reserve Minutes   Indication of a battery's capacity is sometimes given in reserve minutes. Unless otherwise stated, this measurement is the number of minutes a fully charged battery will put out a full 25-amp current before its voltage drops to 10.5.

CONDUCTING ELECTRICITY

The majority of boat electrical systems work on relatively low voltage, which calls for a substantial thickness of good quality copper wire conductor, multi-stranded for resistance to vibration.

Wire that is too thin resists the flow of electricity, leading to a voltage drop at the end of its run. It can even heat up and pose a fire risk.

A voltage drop of 10 percent is permissible for cabin light circuits and other applications where voltage is not critical, but a drop of more than 3 percent should not be tolerated for electronic gear, navigation lights, and so on. Because voltage drops with the length of the conductor, the longer the run, the thicker the wire needed.

American Wire Gauge Tables

American Wire Gauge (AWG) Sizes For a 10-Percent Voltage Drop at 12V DC

Current on Circuit	Feet Run										
	20	30	40	50	60	70	80	90	100	110	120
5 amps	16	16	16	16	14	14	14	14	12	12	12
10 amps	16	14	14	12	12	12	10	10	10	10	8
15 amps	14	14	12	10	10	10	8	8	8	8	8
20 amps	12	12	10	10	8	8	8	6	6	6	6
25 amps	10	10	10	8	8	8	6	6	6	6	4

Note: Feet run is the total length of the wire from the source, to the appliance, and back to the source.

American Wire Gauge (AWG) Sizes For a 3-Percent Voltage Drop at 12V DC

Current on Circuit	Feet Run										
	20	30	40	50	60	70	80	90	100	110	120
5 amps	14	12	12	10	10	8	8	8	8	8	6
10 amps	12	10	8	8	6	6	6	5	5	5	4
15 amps	10	8	6	6	5	5	4	4	3	3	2
20 amps	8	6	6	5	4	3	2	2	2	2	1
25 amps	8	6	5	4	3	3	2	1	1	1	0

American Wire Gauge (AWG) Diameters

AWG	Inches	mm		AWG	Inches	mm
0000	0.46	11.68		6	0.162	4.11
				7	0.144	3.66
000	0.41	10.41		8	0.128	3.25
				9	0.114	2.90
00	0.365	9.27		10	0.102	2.59
				11	0.091	2.31
0	0.325	8.25		12	0.081	2.06
				13	0.072	1.83
1	0.289	7.34		14	0.064	1.63
				15	0.057	1.45
2	0.258	6.55		16	0.051	1.30
				17	0.045	1.14
3	0.229	5.82		18	0.04	1.02
4	0.204	5.18		19	0.036	0.91
5	0.182	4.62		20	0.032	0.81

Note: All gauges refer to the diameter of the wire conductor only; they do not account for insulation.

Color Code for Marine Wiring

American Boat and Yacht Council's Recommendations for DC Systems Under 50V

Color	Use
Brown	Generator armature to regulator; generator terminal/alternator auxiliary terminal to light to regulator; fuse or switch to pumps
Dark Blue	Fuse or switch to cabin and instrument lights
Dark Gray	Fuse or switch to navigation lights; tachometer sender to gauge
Green	Ground or bonding wire
Light Blue	Oil-pressure sender to gauge
Orange	Ammeter to alternator or generator output and accessory fuses or switches; distribution panel to accessory switch
Pink	Fuel-gauge sender to gauge
Purple	Ignition switch to coil and instruments; distribution panel to instruments
Red	Positive main
Tan	Water-temperature sender to gauge
White / Black	Return, negative main. Either color is acceptable, but not a mixture of both.
Yellow	Generator or alternator field to regulator field terminal; bilge blowers; fuse or switch to bilge blowers
Yellow / red stripe	Starting switch to solenoid

Standard Color Codes for 120V AC Wiring

Color	Use
Black	Identifies the "hot," current-carrying line
White	Neutral ground return
Green	Non-current-carrying line grounding a metal cabinet or chassis

Joining Electrical Wires

Many competent authorities now advise that you crimp electrical wires to terminal connections rather than solder them. But the crimping must be done with the correct tool specified by the terminal manufacturer.

After careful cleaning and crimping, the joint should be waterproofed and protected from salt air with an air-drying liquid vinyl or shrink-wrap tubing.

Some marine professionals also advise soldering connections after crimping them. Others believe soldering tends to produce hard spots that cause fatigue and breakage in the wire. In addition, they say, salt air attacks solder, leaving a messy white residue with little strength and dubious electrical integrity.

Use only 100-percent nonferrous terminals, never plated steel—check with a magnet when you purchase—and always test a new connection by pulling hard to make sure the crimp is good.

USING ELECTRICITY

Modern sailboats tend to use more electricity every year. Apart from the normal demand for pressurized water, better lighting, more efficient pumps, and electrical anchor winches, yacht designers are increasingly incorporating bow thrusters and push-button sail reefing in their designs.

The introduction of more efficient inverters (which change the energy in your battery to 110V AC power) has made it possible to use household computers, TV sets, blenders, and power drills on board.

Inverters draw 12V DC current from the ship's batteries and convert it with little loss of efficiency and none of the noise and fumes of the normal gas- or diesel-powered generator.

Selecting an Inverter Inverter output ranges from 50 watts to about 2,500 watts. Choose the right size by figuring maximum wattage draw at any one time. To calculate inverter size from available battery capacity:

Total battery bank amp-hours $\times$ 5 = maximum inverter output in watts.

Thus, a 100-amp-hour battery will comfortably support a 500-watt inverter without the need for constant recharging.

Navigation and Communication Instruments Just as VHF radio has replaced signals flags and semaphore, the falling price of Global Positioning System (GPS) receivers is ousting the sextant among cruising sailors. Little wonder, when you can buy three or four GPS sets for the price of a good sextant. Most authorities warn sailors not to depend solely on GPS, however. Like most man-made systems, it can go wrong somewhere along the line, either up in the heavens where its high-altitude satellites orbit the earth, or right down here in your hand when battery power runs out.

Accuracy of GPS Receivers By comparing time signals from several high-flying satellites, a GPS set will provide you with a fix that is accurate to within about 300 feet. Most receivers track between five and 12 satellites.

The system is inherently able to provide much greater accuracy—to within 50 feet (15 meters)—but the U.S. Department of Defense intentionally degrades the system, supposedly in an attempt to prevent enemies from tak-

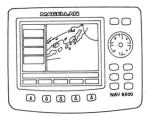

ing advantage of it. When the Department of Defense is activating this so-called Selective Availability (SA), the system gives 300-foot (100-meter) accuracy, or better, 95 percent of the time and 1,000-foot (300-meter) accuracy, or better, 99.99 percent of the time.

But ironically, another U.S. government branch is using taxpayers' money to outwit the Department of Defense and restore full accuracy to GPS. The Coast Guard is building Differential GPS (DGPS) transmitters around the U.S. coastline. They compare the degraded GPS signals with known site positions, and transmit a correction factor to all GPS receivers within range.

Thus, DGPS should be accurate to within 50 feet (15 meters) at all times, no matter how much the Department of Defense degrades its signal, as long as the GPS set is within range of a Coast Guard DGPS station operating on the beacon band from 285 to 325 kHz, and as long as the GPS is connected to a special differential beacon receiver. Differential correction is also available for an annual fee from private commercial firms, using "empty" portions of existing FM/VHF radio bands.

Note: While GPS provides excellent accuracy worldwide, it is important to understand that many current nautical charts use coordinate systems that differ from the GPS standard by unknown amounts. This means that coordinates of latitude and longitude given by a GPS may be inaccurate by amounts varying from a few yards to several miles when plotted on a paper chart.

GPS should therefore be used with caution when approaching a hazard from seaward, and the vessel's true position should be ascertained as soon as possible by radar or from bearings of visible charted landmarks.

Accuracy of Loran Receivers

Loran has the ability to return with great accuracy to a waypoint it has visited before—so much so, that fishermen use it to return to fishing spots only yards in diameter.

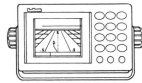

Its geographic accuracy is normally within about 440 yards (400 meters). Daytime reception is often good 500 miles out to sea, and that range just about doubles at night. Some units claim 220-yard (200-meter) accuracy and a range of 700 nautical miles.

Loran or GPS?

	GPS	Loran
PROS	Worldwide coverage Accurate to within 100 yards (100 m) or 50 feet (15 m) with DPGS	Better repeatable accuracy Accurate to within 220 yards (200 m)
CONS	Subject to signal degrading by Department of Defense	Coverage not worldwide

Electronic Charts   When connected to a GPS or loran set, electronic charts give a graphic display of a nautical chart with your boat's position displayed on it.

Digitized charts, sometimes lacking some of the detail on traditional charts, are available for most of the world. Chart cartridges store from six to 90 ordinary charts.

The chart may be displayed on a GPS plotter screen; on the cathode ray tube (CRT) screen of a personal computer (giving good resolution of about 672×512 pixels); on a pocket calculator-sized liquid-crystal display (LCD) screen; or on the screen of a laptop computer with resolution of 160×160 or 240×320 pixels.

Radar   Radar for small sailboats comes with compact LCD screens and scales from 220 yards (200 meters) to 16 nautical miles. Horizontal beam width is typically 6 degrees and vertical beam width 30 degrees. This means a radar transmission from a sailboat heeling 15 degrees or more will be aimed at the sky unless the revolving antenna is mounted in a self-leveling radome. Current draw is usually about 10 watts or less in power-economy mode.

Ranges of Radio Transmitters   Single sideband (SSB) radiotelephones work in the 2 MHz to 22 MHz bands. Very High Frequency (VHF) radios in the marine band work on 156 to 162 MHz.

Frequency allocations. Ham radio frequencies in black.

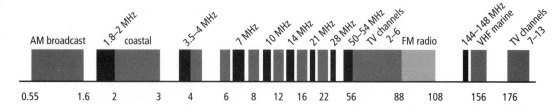

Ranges of SSB Radios

2 MHz:	100 to 150 miles in daylight; 100 to 300 miles at night.
4 MHz:	250 miles (day); 150 to 1,000 miles (night).
6 MHz:	50 to 100 miles (day); 250 to 1,800 miles (night).
8 MHz:	250 to 500 miles (day); 300 to 3,000 (night).
12 MHz:	400 to 4,000 miles, late afternoon and all night.
16 MHz:	1,000 to 6,000 miles day and night, but best during the day.
22 MHz:	1,200 to 8,000 miles or more day and night, but unpredictable and dependent on propagation conditions.

Ranges of VHF Radios

VHF range is essentially line-of-sight, and depends on the heights of the transmitting and receiving antennas. This table gives ranges in nautical miles.

Height of Receiving Antenna	Height of Transmitting Antenna			
	4 Ft. (1.2 m)	20 Ft. (6 m)	40 Ft. (12 m)	60 Ft. (18 m)
0	2.3	5.1	7.3	8.9
8 ft. (2.4 m)	5.6	8.4	10.5	12.2
20 ft. (6 m)	7.4	10.3	12.4	14.1
50 ft. (15 m)	10.4	13.3	15.4	17.0
100 ft. (30 m)	13.8	16.6	18.8	20.4
200 ft. (61 m)	18.6	21.4	23.5	25.2
400 ft. (122 m)	25.3	28.1	30.3	31.9
1,000 ft. (305 m)	38.7	41.5	43.6	45.3

VHF Antenna Gain (dB Rating)

The dB rating of antennas indicates the pattern in which the radio wave energy is transmitted. Short antennas (up to 5 feet or 1.5 m) transmit in all directions at once. They are commonly described as having a dB rating of 0 to 3 though, strictly speaking, that is not technically correct.

Longer antennas (8 to 17 feet, or 2 to 5 m) have a rating of 6 to 10 dB, compressing radiation into a flatter pattern flowing out at right angles from the antenna. In so doing, they strengthen the signal at the receiving point by 4 to 10 times.

But a right-angled transmission from a heeled sailboat would be aimed at the sky or the water, rather than the horizon.

Most authorities agree, therefore, that the best VHF antenna for sailboats has a 3-dB gain, which almost doubles signal strength at the receiving end, but still allows transmission horizontally when the boat is heeled.

A 3-dB antenna may be mounted on the transom, but for greater range it should be mounted at the masthead.

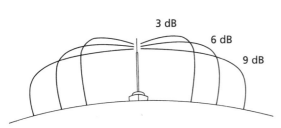

High-gain antennas "flatten" the radiation pattern, increasing the signal at low angles.

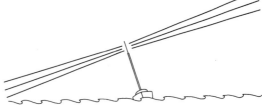

The radiation pattern from an antenna with too much gain may be directed largely into the sky or water, causing fading and bad reception.

VHF Marine Channels

Some VHF channels are assigned exclusively to commercial vessels, others exclusively to noncommercial (recreational) vessels, and some channels may be used by both.

Channel Number	Designated Use
16	Distress, safety, and calling (Ship to ship, or ship to shore)
09	Alternative calling (Ship to ship)
06	Safety messages (Between ships)
07, 10, 11, 18, 19, 79, 80	Commercial vessels only (Between ships and ship to shore)
08, 67, 77, 78	Commercial vessels only (Between ships)
12, 14, 20, 65, 66, 73, 74	Port operations (Ship to ship, and ship to shore)
13	Navigation messages (Between ships, and ship to shore)
22	Coast Guard liaison and marine safety broadcasts (Between ships, shore, and aircraft)
24, 25, 26, 27,28, 84, 85, 86, 87, 88	Public correspondence (Ship-to-shore radiotelephone)
68, 69, 71, 78	Noncommercial (pleasure boats) only (Between ships, and ship to shore)
70	Digital selective calling only (Between ships, and ship to shore)
72	Noncommercial (pleasure boats) only (Between ships)

Signal Loss in Coaxial Cable

Signals moving from your transmitter to the antenna are weakened by the coax cable along which they pass. Like any other conductor, a coax cable must be appropriately sized for the distance it spans.

This table shows approximate dB losses for different-sized cables. A loss of 3 dB will halve the signal strength. Losses of 4 dB and 6 dB will reduce signal strength by about two-thirds and three-quarters respectively.

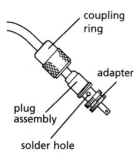

coupling ring

adapter

plug assembly

solder hole

Cable Type	Diameter (approx.)		Loss per 100 Feet Run		Maximum Run	
RG-58	3/16 in.	5 mm	6.1 dB	75%	49 ft.	15 m
RG-8X	1/4 in.	6 mm	4.5 dB	65%	66 ft.	20 m
RG-8U	3/8 in.	10 mm	2.7 dB	46%	111 ft.	34 m

Radio Frequency and Wavelength

Frequency is measured in cycles per second, or Hertz, named after German physicist Heinrich Rudolph Hertz. One kilohertz (kHz) = 1,000 cycles a second, and one megahertz (MHz) = 1,000,000 cycles per second.

The length of radio waves is measured in meters, and groups of frequencies are still often referred to as bands, named by wavelength in meters.

Frequency (in MHz) and wavelength (in meters) bear a fixed relationship to each other—the "300" rule.

Frequency to wavelength: Divide 300 by MHz to convert to meters.

Wavelength to frequency: Divide 300 by meters to convert to MHz.

Examples:

1. 4 MHz = 300 ÷ 4 = 75 meters.
2. 15 meters = 300 ÷ 15 = 20 MHz.

Depthsounders

Depthsounders measure the time it takes a sound signal to travel to the sea bed and back, from which they calculate water depth.

Transducers for pleasure craft usually work with a signal frequency of 50 or 200 kHz, although 75-kHz transducers are becoming more popular. Lower frequencies penetrate water better, so a 50-kHz transducer will give readings in deeper water. The higher-frequency 200-kHz transducers provide more detail for fish finders.

Expect maximum depth readings in salt water to be 25 percent to 50 percent less than the manufacturers' claims, which are usually based on maximum depth soundings achieved in fresh water.

Depending on the hull material and method of installation, transducers installed inside the hull also can substantially reduce the sounder's maximum depth-reading ability.

Emergency Position-Indicating Radio Beacons (EPIRBs)

Class A: Transmits on 121.5 and 243.0 MHz. Automatically floats free of its mount and turns itself on.

Class B: Transmits on 121.5 and 243.0 MHz. Must be turned on manually.

Category I: Transmits on 406 and 121.5 MHz. Automatically floats free of its mount and turns itself on.

Category II: Transmits on 406 and 121.5 MHz. Must be turned on manually.

Confusingly, the federal government now also subdivides Category I and Category II (406 MHz) EPIRBs into Class 1 and Class 2. Class 1 EPIRBs are designed to work in cold temperatures, down to −40°F (−40°C). Class 2 EPIRBs are suitable where temperatures do not drop below −4°F (−20°C).

Class A and B (243 MHz) EPIRBs cost about a third of the price of Category I and II (406 MHz) EPIRBs, but are effective only when a receiving satellite is also in line of sight with a ground receiving station, most of which are in the northern hemisphere. This means emergency signals may not be picked up immediately—or even before the batteries run down—from boats in trouble in the southern hemisphere and other parts of the world.

Emergency messages from Category I and II (406 MHz) EPIRBs are recorded by satellites which retransmit them when they are within range of a ground station, thus ensuring worldwide coverage. Their signals also are coded to identify your boat and provide details helpful to rescuers. For this purpose, it is vital to register Category I and II (406 MHz) EPIRBs in the United States. Manufacturers include registration forms with the beacons and the National Oceanic and Atmospheric Administration (NOAA) issues a decal to indicate that the EPIRB is registered.

More accurate positions are provided by 406 MHz EPIRBs—often within a 2-mile radius—than by the Class A and B (243 MHz) models, which guide rescuers to within 10 or 15 miles, after which it is possible to home in on the simultaneous 121.5 MHz transmission.

Most EPIRBs will transmit for at least 48 hours.

 EPIRB batteries have a useful life of 10 to 12 years but should be replaced at least every five years.

Lightning Protection A grounded vertical metal conductor 10 feet (3 m) high for every 17 feet (5 m) of boat length will attract and divert lightning flashes, thus providing a boat with a cone of protection angled downward at 120 degrees from the top of the conductor.

A sailboat's metal mast makes a good conductor. A wooden mast will need at least #4 AWG stranded (not solid) copper wire, or copper strip at least 1/32 (0.8 mm) inch thick, projecting at least 6 inches (150 mm) above the mast. This conductor, or a metal mast, must be connected as directly as possible (that is, with as few bends as possible) to a lightning ground connection—a submerged grounding surface of at least 1 square foot (0.1 square meters).

Standing rigging, as well as any winches, guardrails, pulpits, and large metallic objects that are not tied into the bonding system should be joined to the ground plate with interconnecting conductors, also stranded, of at least #8 AWG.

120° cone
of protection

copper tube (3/4 in.) or copper
wire (#4) directly from mast

ground plate

Engines

Fuel Consumption of Inboard Engines

Because fuel consumption varies with speed, the following table refers to horsepower *used* at any given time, not maximum horsepower available from the engine. Most marine engines are designed to run continuously at 60 to 80 percent of maximum speed, and diesels tend toward the top of the range.

U.S. Gallons / Liters Consumed

Engine Type	Gallons per Hour	per hp	liter/hr/kW
Gasoline, 4-cycle	1 per 10 hp	0.090	0.458
Gasoline, 2-cycle	1 per 8 to 9 hp	0.100	0.509
Diesel, 4-cycle	1 per 18 hp	0.055	0.280

Only about 13 or 14 percent of your fuel's energy is available to turn the propeller. This is where the rest goes.

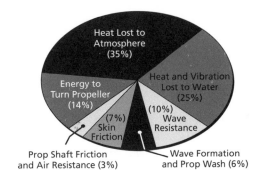

Heat Lost to Atmosphere (35%)

Energy to Turn Propeller (14%)

Heat and Vibration Lost to Water (25%)

(7%) Skin Friction

(10%) Wave Resistance

Prop Shaft Friction and Air Resistance (3%)

Wave Formation and Prop Wash (6%)

Consumption by Fuel Weight

By and large, gasoline inboard engines need 0.6 pound of fuel, and diesel engines 0.4 pound, to produce one horsepower (or 365 g to produce 1 kW) for one hour.

Fuel Energy Content

On average, diesel fuel contains about 140,000 British thermal units (Btu) per U.S. gallon, or 10 percent more energy than the same volume of gasoline.

Fuel Weights

Diesel weighs about 7.1 pounds per U.S. gallon (840 g/liter).
Gasoline weighs about 6.1 pounds per U.S. gallon (730 g/liter).

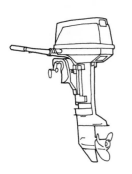

Fuel Consumption of Outboard Engines

Because of fuel waste associated with the scavenging of exhaust gases, two-cycle gasoline outboards invariably use more fuel than inboard gas engines or four-cycle outboards. Precise comparisons of fuel efficiency between inboards and outboards are difficult, and perhaps irrelevant, because often there is no choice about what type or size of engine will suit a particular boat.

It is fairly safe to assume, however, that a two-cycle outboard can be 10 to 50 percent thirstier than an inboard gasoline engine of comparable horsepower.

The rule of thumb given above for the fuel consumption of two-cycle gasoline inboard engines (0.100 U.S. gallon/hour/hp, or 0.509 liter/hour/kW) is also valid for most two-cycle outboards driving displacement hulls at less than maximum hull speed.

A new generation of fuel-injected two-cycle outboards is expected to improve fuel consumption considerably.

Four-cycle gasoline outboards are more economical than their two-cycle cousins, and diesel outboards are better still.

POWER REQUIREMENTS FOR VARIOUS SPEEDS

The speed of planing dinghies and powerboats is determined almost wholly by the power available. It's the power-to-weight ratio that counts. For example, a planing hull can achieve 25 knots with an all-up weight (boat, fuel, crew, stores, everything) of 40 pounds for every 1 horsepower delivered to the propeller. Change that 40:1 ratio to 10:1—that is, 10 pounds for every 1 horsepower—and the speed goes up to 50 knots. A hull trim angle between 2 and 4 degrees bows-up from horizontal minimizes resistance while planing.

On the other hand, most sailboats have displacement-type hulls, which restrict their maximum speed to approximately the speed of the wave they create.

 A displacement hull's maximum speed in knots is determined by calculating

the square root of the boat's waterline length in feet × 1.34,

OR

the square root of the waterline length in meters × 2.43.

Inboard Engine Speed/Hp Graph for Small Yachts

(Waterline lengths from 16 to 30 feet [4.8 m to 9 m])

Key to waterline lengths:
A = 16 ft. (4.8 m)
B = 18 ft. (5.5 m)
C = 20 ft. (6 m)
D = 22 ft. (6.7 m)
E = 24 ft. (7.3 m)
F = 26 ft. (8 m)
G = 30 ft. (9 m)

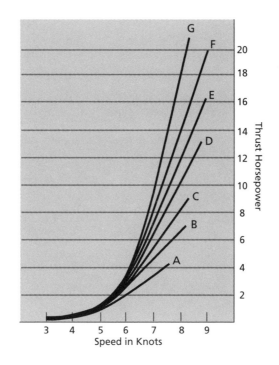

Inboard Engine Speed/Hp Graph for Larger Yachts

(Waterline lengths from 30 feet to 50 feet [9 m to 15 m])

Key to waterline lengths:
H = 30 ft. (9 m)
J = 35 ft. (10.7 m)
K = 40 ft. (12 m)
L = 45 ft. (13.7 m)
M = 50 ft. (15.2 m)

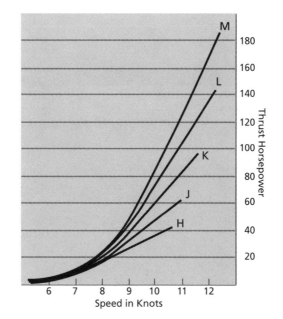

Outboard Engine Power Required in Small Auxiliary Sailboats

This graph applies to boats with waterline lengths of up to 20 feet.

➤ It indicates hull speed in calm conditions for boats with average windage and hull/keel shapes.

➤ Heavy winds and waves will cause speeds to drop substantially.

➤ For all-weather work, substantially larger engines might be needed—even twice as large as those indicated here.

➤ Racing boats with little resistance and light displacement may need slightly less power.

➤ Heavily laden cruising boats, especially those with a lot of top hamper, will almost certainly need more power.

➤ Efficiency depends as much on the correct propeller turning at the correct speed as on horsepower.

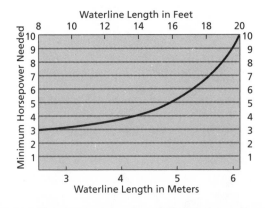

OUTBOARD ENGINE WEIGHTS

These are typical weights of popular two-cycle (or two-stroke) gasoline outboard engines suitable for dinghies and small sailboats.

Horsepower	Displacement cc	Approximate Weight	
		Pounds	kg
2.5	75	28	13
3.5	75	28	13
5	100	45	20
6	145	51	23
8	170	55	25
9.9	250	85	38
15	250	85	38

Note: An empty 6-gallon (23-liter) portable fuel tank for an outboard motor weighs about 11 pounds (5 kg). Filled with gasoline, at 6.1 pounds to the gallon (0.73 kg/liter), it weighs nearly 48 pounds (22 kg).

Gas/Oil Mixture for Two-Cycle Outboard Engines

Older two-cycle engines without automatic oil injection require lubricant pre-mixed into the gasoline. The fuel/oil ratio depends on the age and make of the engine, and may vary from 16:1 to 100:1.

Fuel Mixing Chart

Gas:Oil Ratio	Ounces of Oil to Add to Gallons of Gasoline					
	1	2	3	4	5	6
16:1	8 oz.	16 oz.	24 oz.	32 oz.	40 oz.	48 oz.
20:1	6	13	19	26	32	38
25:1	5	10	15	20	26	31
50:1	3	5	8	11	13	16
100:1	2	3	4	6	7	8

Note: The recommended lubricating oil is designated TC-W (for two-cycle, water-cooled engines.) The procedure for mixing the oil and gasoline varies with the temperature and the kind of gas tank:

Above 32°F (0°C):

Portable tank: Pour the oil into the tank and add gasoline. Replace the filler cap, turn the tank on its side, then return it to the upright position again.

Fixed tank: Pour the oil in slowly with the gasoline.

Below 32°F (0°C):

Portable tank: Pour about a gallon (4 liters) of gas into the tank. Add all the oil. Replace the filler cap and shake the container thoroughly. Add the balance of the gas.

Fixed tank: Mix oil and about a gallon (4 liters) of gas in a separate container. Pour this mixture slowly into the tank as the rest of the gas is added.

MINIMUM SIZES FOR INBOARD ENGINE VENTS

Engine compartments without forced-air ventilation need a steady supply of cool, dry, clean air. The collective size of the vents varies according to the horsepower of the engine:

Minimum vent area in square inches = horsepower ÷ 3.3.

Minimum vent area in square centimeters = kW × 2.6.

This formula for natural ventilation includes an allowance for air-flow obstructions found in a regular installation, such as standard grilles and louvers.

Example:

A 40-horsepower diesel without forced-air ventilation will need a minimum vent area of 12 square inches (7,742 mm²). This could be provided, say, by one vent with a diameter of 4 inches (100 mm) or by two vents, each with a diameter of 3 inches (75 mm).

ENGINE-MOUNTING BOLTS

Properly mounted engines are fitted to heavy steel or aluminum angle stock through-bolted to the engine beds or stringers.

Engine stringer at engine.

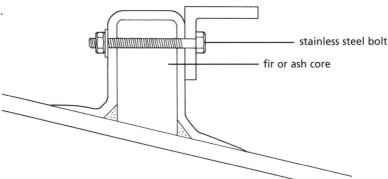

stainless steel bolt

fir or ash core

Each angle should be fastened through its side to its stringer with four bolts.

Each bolt should have a minimum diameter, in inches, of the total engine weight in pounds divided by 4,000. (Or a minimum diameter, in millimeters, of engine weight in kg divided by 70.) The minimum bolt diameter is ³/₈ inch (10 mm). The engine mounts should be bolted through the top of the angle.

ENGINE-BED SIZE

A safe standard for wooden and fiberglass hulls is to make the molding, or width measured athwartships, of each engine bearer a minimum of ¹/₄₀ of the boat's overall beam. The depth should be the same as the molding, except at the engine itself, where, from mount to mount, the bearer depth should be increased by 50 percent.

On glass hulls, the engine stringers should run for most of the length of the boat, especially in powerboats.

Propellers

Choosing the right propeller is as much an art as a science. Even naval architects sometimes have to resort to trial and error, although they do at least know where to start and how to improve matters. Very few new designs are delivered with perfect propellers.

This graph gives a rough indication of where to begin. It will certainly tell you if your present prop is drastically unsuitable. It's a nomograph prepared by naval architect and author Dave Gerr, and it's valid for three-bladed props. The diameter of a two-bladed propeller of equivalent thrust would be approximately 5 percent greater.

Note that the column marked "Rpm" refers to the turning speed of the propeller, not the engine. If you have a reduction gear, make the appropriate allowance.

Example:

1. Your owner's manual says your reduction gear ratio is 26:15.

2. That means when the engine turns over at 2,600 rpm, the propeller spins at 1,500 rpm.

3. Therefore, propeller speed is always 1,500/2,600, or 15/26, of engine speed.

4. For example, at 1,800-rpm engine speed, propeller speed is $1,800 \times (15 \div 26) = 1,038$ rpm.

To estimate propeller diameter, lay a straight-edge from shaft rpm to shaft hp. This graph is for standard three-bladed propellers with a 50-percent disc/area ratio. (Prepared by Dave Gerr and used courtesy of International Marine, Camden, ME, from *The Nature of Boats*.)

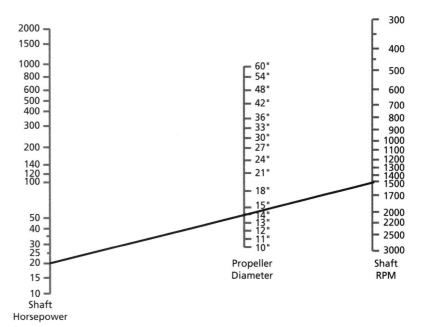

PROPELLERS

45

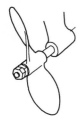

➤ Propellers for auxiliary sailboats are usually two-bladed or three-bladed. The majority are fixed but others will feather, fold, or change their pitch under way.

➤ A two-bladed propeller is the most efficient for most sailboats, but often there just isn't sufficient clearance between the shaft and the hull to accommodate the long, thin blades, so a smaller-diameter, three-bladed prop must be used instead.

➤ When a boat is sailing, a two-bladed prop that can be lined up vertically behind the rudder post causes less resistance in the water than does a three-bladed prop.

➤ A three-bladed prop is less prone to vibration, however, and needs a smaller hole in the rudder, if that's the way it's fitted. But each blade of a three-bladed prop works in water slightly more disturbed by its predecessor than does the blade of a two-bladed prop, so it's slightly less efficient and also has a less beneficial aspect ratio.

➤ A folding prop, two-bladed or three-bladed, causes very little drag, but is more suited to a racing boat than a cruiser because it may not work efficiently if it is not used very frequently. One barnacle growing in the wrong place could prevent it from opening properly. Folding props depend on centrifugal force to fling the blades open, and are often very poor performers in astern gear.

➤ Adjustable-pitch props need neither gearbox nor clutch, but the sophisticated mechanism needed to vary the pitch under way is expensive and prone to malfunction. They are therefore quite rare. Recent experiments with props that adjust their pitch automatically under power and offer minimal resistance under sail have proved very promising, but there are still problems to be solved.

➤ Automatic feathering props, such as the Max-Prop, greatly reduce drag while sailing and improve performance during a long voyage under sail. But fine engineering makes them too expensive for most boatowners.

PROPELLER PITCH / RPM / SLIPPAGE

The pitch of a propeller is the distance it would advance through the water in one revolution if there were no slippage. In practice, the amount of slippage for most auxiliary sailboats is between 40 and 55 percent of that distance, the figure rising with heavier displacement boats. For high-speed planing powerboats, the slippage figure is about 20 percent. For trawler-type powerboats it is about 26 percent.

PROPELLERS

The graph below should be entered at the top with the approximate percentage of propeller slip, as given above. Drop straight down to the northwest/southeast diagonal line representing your boat speed. From this position, move horizontally to meet the vertical line drawn upward from the shaft rpm. At this final position, note the closest diagonal running northeast/southwest, which represents the correct pitch in inches.

For an auxiliary sailboat, boat speed may be taken as 90 percent of theoretical top hull speed or 90 percent of the estimated maximum speed available from the engine.

Note that speed is given in mph. To convert mph to knots, multiply mph by 7 and divide the result by 8. To convert knots to mph, multiply knots by 8 and divide the result by 7.

How to Find Propeller Pitch

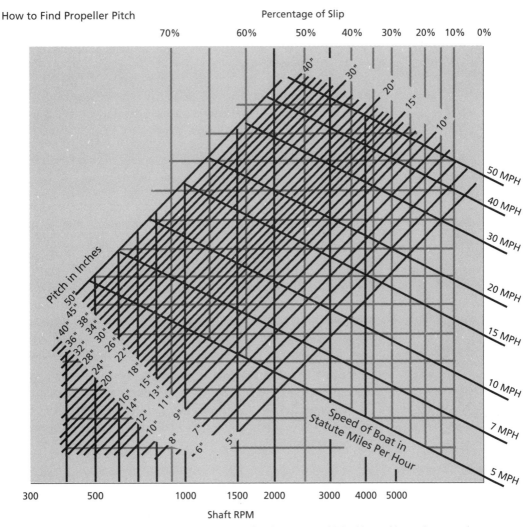

Chart by George F. Crouch, from *Skene's Elements of Yacht Design*, published by Dodd, Mead, New York.

➤ By convention, propeller diameter is marked first, followed by pitch. A 12-
× 13-inch propeller has a diameter of 12 inches and a pitch of 13 inches.

➤ Increased diameter absorbs more power than does increased pitch.

➤ A decrease of 1 inch (25 mm) in propeller diameter will increase engine
rpm by about 300.

➤ On auxiliary sailboats, minimum clearance around the tips of the propeller blades is 10 percent of propeller diameter.

➤ Powerboats need 20 percent or more clearance to avoid vibration.

➤ Because colder water is denser, propeller diameter should be reduced
about 1 percent for every 10°F (5.6°C) drop in water temperature, based
on a "normal" of 70°F (21°C).

➤ After installing a propeller on a shaft, put the thinner nut on first, and
allow the larger nut, with more thread area, to assume the load when it is
tightened up against the thin locknut.

➤ For greatest efficiency, the pitch-to-diameter ratio should be less than
1.4 : 1, except on high-speed (35 knots plus) boats.

➤ A large-diameter propeller is always more efficient than a smaller one,
except on boats that are designed for continuous operation at 35 knots or
more.

➤ There is disagreement among the experts about whether a prop free to
rotate under sail causes less drag than one that is fixed. U.S. naval architect
Dave Gerr says flatly: "The simple answer is that a propeller creates less
drag when free to rotate." British author Eric Hiscock says: "Experiments
made by P. Newall Petticrow Ltd. have shown that a 2- or 3-bladed propeller offers less drag when it is locked than when it is free to spin, and that
the drag of a spinning propeller is greatest at about 100 rpm." Another
American naval architect, Francis S. Kinney, agrees with Hiscock. "The
shaft should be locked," he writes in *Skene's Elements of Yacht Design*, "so
that the propeller cannot revolve. It has been found that a revolving propeller creates more drag . . ."

PROPELLERS

PROPELLER BLADE AREA

Cavitation occurs when too much horsepower is forced into too small a propeller, that is, when blade loading is too high. This formula was derived by naval architect Dave Gerr from projected boat speed in knots, and gives the minimum blade area (total area of all blades) needed to avoid cavitation:

Area in square inches $= (100 \times$ shaft hp$) \div ($knots $\times \sqrt{\text{knots}})$.

Area in square centimeters $= (865 \times$ shaft kW$) \div ($knots $\times \sqrt{\text{knots}})$.

CONVERTING FROM THREE-BLADED PROPELLERS

Diameter and pitch vary with the number of propeller blades. A propeller modified as follows will perform about the same as the original:

To change from three blades to two, multiply diameter by 1.05 and pitch by 1.01.

To change from three blades to four, multiply diameter by 0.94 and pitch by 0.98.

PROPELLER SHAFT DIAMETER

These recommended minimum sizes, in inches, are for bronze shafting. The diameter of stainless steel shafts may be reduced by 10 percent. Note that the slower the prop's maximum rpm for a given horsepower, the thicker the shaft must be to handle the increased torque.

	Propeller Shaft Maximum Rpm				
BHP	3,000	2,000	1,500	1,000	500
3	1/2	9/16	5/8	11/16	7/8
6	5/8	11/16	3/4	7/8	1 1/8
10	11/16	13/16	7/8	1 1/16	1 5/16
20	7/8	1 1/16	1 1/8	1 5/16	1 5/8
30	1 1/16	1 3/16	1 5/16	1 1/2	1 7/8
40	1 1/8	1 5/16	1 7/16	1 5/8	2 1/16
50	1 1/4	1 3/8	1 9/16	1 3/4	2 1/4
75	1 3/8	1 5/8	1 3/4	2	2 9/16
100	1 9/16	1 3/4	1 15/16	2 1/4	2 13/16
125	1 11/16	1 15/16	2 1/16	2 3/8	3
150	1 3/4	2	2 1/4	2 9/16	3 1/4

Shaft size may also be estimated for small craft by using these old rules of thumb:

➤ For a bronze shaft, divide propeller diameter by 14.5 for a two-bladed prop and by 14 for a three-bladed prop.

➤ For a stainless steel shaft, subtract 10 percent of the size given for bronze.

➤ For a Monel shaft, divide propeller diameter by 18.1 for a two-bladed prop and by 17.5 for a three-bladed prop.

Example:

1. Diameter of three-bladed propeller is 15 inches.
2. Diameter of a suitable bronze shaft must be 15 ÷ 14 = 1.07 inches.
3. Diameter of a stainless steel shaft must be 1.07 minus 10 percent (0.107) = 0.963 inches.
4. Diameter of a Monel shaft must be 15 ÷ 1.75 = 0.86 inches.

PITCH / DIAMETER RELATIONSHIP

 For roughly equivalent performance, if you decrease the diameter of a propeller 1 inch, you should increase its pitch 2 inches.

PROPELLER SHAFT BEARINGS

To remain straight, a propeller shaft needs to be supported at intervals along its length. Bearings should be no closer to each other than 20 times the shaft diameter, and no farther apart than shown here:

Shaft Diameter		Bearing Spacing	
3/4 in.	19 mm	4 ft. 0 in.	1.22 m
7/8 in.	22 mm	4 ft. 4 in.	1.32 m
1 in.	25 mm	4 ft. 7 in.	1.40 m
1 1/8 in.	28 mm	4 ft. 10 in.	1.47 m
1 1/4 in.	32 mm	5 ft. 1 in.	1.55 m
1 3/8 in.	35 mm	5 ft. 4 in.	1.63 m
1 1/2 in.	38 mm	5 ft. 8 in.	1.73 m
1 5/8 in.	41 mm	5 ft. 10 in.	1.78 m
1 3/4 in.	44 mm	6 ft. 1 in.	1.85 m
1 7/8 in.	48 mm	6 ft. 4 in.	1.93 m
2 in.	51 mm	6 ft. 6 in.	1.98 m
2 1/4 in.	57 mm	6 ft. 11 in.	2.11 m
2 1/2 in.	64 mm	7 ft. 4 in.	2.23 m
2 3/4 in.	70 mm	7 ft. 8 in.	2.34 m
3 in.	76 mm	8 ft. 0 in.	2.44 m

Fiberglass

The glass fabrics most commonly used by boatbuilders are cloth, woven roving, and chopped strand mat.

➤ Cloth is thin and strong. It is used for sheathing wood or as a finishing layer on a glass laminate because it gives a smooth finish. It is not often used in hull laminates.

➤ Woven roving has a loose weave with a rough finish. It provides strength but is usually topped with cloth or mat to make it fair.

➤ Mat comprises short strands of glass fiber laid flat in random fashion and held in place by a sizing soluble in resin. It is the weakest of these three fabrics, but it bonds well. In repair work, it is the fabric first applied to old fiberglass.

Chopped strand mat

Cloth

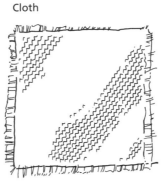

Woven roving

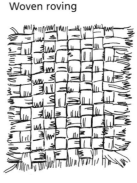

STANDARD BOATBUILDING LAMINATE

Most production-run fiberglass boats are built of this laminate: Alternating layers of chopped-strand mat at 1.5 ounces to the square yard and woven roving at 24 ounces to the square yard. In metric terms, that's 48 g/m² mat and 780 g/m² roving. The standard resin is polyester. These two layers are called a ply, and each ply is about 3/32 inch (2.38 mm) thick.

This laminate weighs about 94 pounds a cubic foot (1.5 kg/m³) and the glass fibers account for about 35 percent of the total weight.

It's useful to be able to estimate whether a hull is strong enough. Here's a rule of thumb from naval architect and yacht designer Dave Gerr:

For solid fiberglass hulls,

$$\text{Skin thickness in inches} = 0.07 + (\text{WL in feet} \div 150).$$

$$\text{Skin thickness in millimeters} = 1.8 + (\text{WL in meters} \div 1.8).$$

Note: These thicknesses are for the middle of the topsides. For the upper topsides, the hull may be 15 percent thinner. For the bottom of the hull, the thickness should be 15 percent greater.

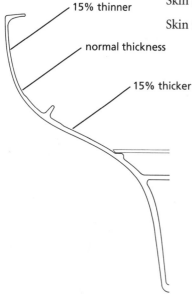

15% thinner

normal thickness

15% thicker

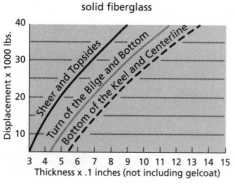

solid fiberglass

Displacement x 1000 lbs.

Sheer and Topsides

Turn of the Bilge and Bottom

Bottom of the Keel and Centerline

Thickness x .1 inches (not including gelcoat)

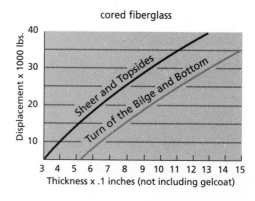

cored fiberglass

Displacement x 1000 lbs.

Sheer and Topsides

Turn of the Bilge and Bottom

Thickness x .1 inches (not including gelcoat)

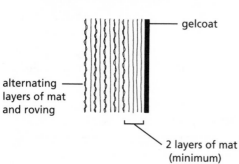

gelcoat

alternating layers of mat and roving

2 layers of mat (minimum)

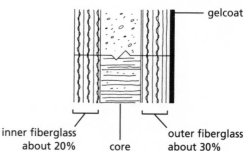

gelcoat

inner fiberglass about 20%

core

outer fiberglass about 30%

FIBERGLASS

To provide stiffness without unnecessary thickness, solid fiberglass hulls built to the above specifications need five or more interior longitudinal stringers evenly spaced on each side. One stringer should be placed at the turn of the bilge. Two others should be equally spaced between the turn of the bilge and the sheer. The last two should be equally spaced between the turn of the bilge and the center of the keel.

Powerboats with engine-bed stringers will not need the two lowest stringers.

In addition to the stringers, at least five structural bulkheads should be evenly spaced throughout the length of the hull.

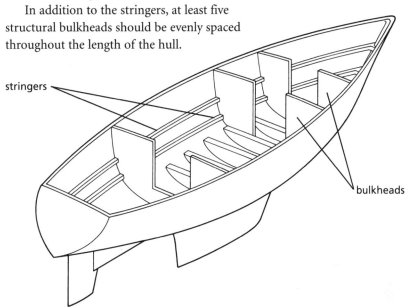

stringers

bulkheads

Foam sandwich or balsa-cored hulls are thicker than solid fiberglass, but about eight times stiffer for the same weight of fiberglass. To find the required thickness of a sandwich-construction hull, first find the thickness of a solid fiberglass hull, as shown above. Then:

➤ The core of foam or balsa should be 2.2 times the solid-hull thickness.

➤ The outer fiberglass skin should be 0.4 times the solid-hull thickness.

➤ The inner fiberglass skin should be 0.3 times the solid-hull thickness.

Note: The core thickness usually remains the same throughout, but the thicknesses of the inner and outer skins should vary—for upper topsides, middle topsides, and bottom—according to the formula given above for a solid fiberglass hull.

FIBERGLASS

53

The glass most used in marine fiberglass layups is known as *E-glass*. Another, higher-quality glass fiber known as *S-glass,* or structural glass, is extruded with much finer strands. It's much stronger and somewhat stiffer than E-glass but costs about twice as much.

Here is a comparison of the strengths and weights of the fibers used to fabricate hulls, decks, superstructures, and spars, compared with steel and aluminum. Also shown is the material's comparative stiffness, that is, its springiness, or resistance to bending, as determined by Young's Modulus of Elasticity (MoE), where the designated fiber forms about 40 percent of the total laminate—a typical amount.

Material	Tensile Strength		Stiffness (MoE)		Weight	
	lb./sq. in.	kg/cm²	lb./sq. in.	kg/cm²	lb./cu. ft.	kg/m³
Carbon fiber	170,000	11,952	1,290,000	906,982	100	1,601
S-Glass	128,000	9,000	5,500,000	386,698	95	1,521
Kevlar	90,000	6,328	3,200,000	224,988	80	1,281
Steel	60,000	4,219	30,000,000	2,109,260	495	7,925
Aluminum	40,000	2,812	10,400,000	731,210	168	2,690
E-Glass	15,000	1,050	1,400,000	98,430	95	1,521

The major factor governing the use of a specific resin is its compatibility with the sizing on the strengthening fiber to be used.

Generally, polyester resin is best with E-glass and S-glass. Vinylester resin and epoxy resin can be used on all fibers.

Most production-run fiberglass layups are made with polyester resin, but the best repairs, postproduction alterations, and additions are made with epoxy resin because epoxy adheres better to fully cured polyester and to wood than does polyester resin.

Vinylester resin is increasingly being used in hull laminations below the waterline, because its greater impermeability helps prevent blistering, or osmosis. And it is usually specified to replace the gelcoat in osmosis repairs.

Wood for Boats

In this table, the strength of each wood is compared with the strength of oak, which is rated at 100.

Name	Weight lb/ft³	Strength	Resistance to rot	Ease of Working	Hardness	Uses
Ash	42	110	Fair	Easy	Very hard	Oars, frames, knees and veneers.
Cedar	28	65	Excellent	Easy	Soft	Planking
Cypress	37	79	Excellent	Easy	Mod. soft	Planking
Douglas fir (Oregon pine)	37	86	Good	Moderate	Mod. soft	Decking, spars, planking
Larch	38	85	Fair	Moderate	Mod. soft	Planking, decking, knees
Mahogany	37	90	Fair	Moderate	Hard	Trim, planking, knees, veneers
Oak, white	48	100	Moderate	Easy	Hard	Frames, knees
Pine, white	27	60	Fair	Easy	Soft	Decking, planking
Spruce	26	66	Fair	Easy	Soft	Spars, oars
Teak	43	85	Excellent	Easy	Mod. soft	Decking, planking, interior trim

APPROXIMATE WEIGHTS OF PLANKING AND CORE MATERIALS

Thickness	Weight in Pounds per Square Foot		
	Fir, Mahogany Pine, Plywood	Teak	Balsa or Foam Core
⅛ in.	0.33	0.47	0.08
¼ in.	0.67	0.94	0.10
⅜ in.	1.00	1.41	0.16
½ in.	1.33	1.88	0.21
⅝ in.	1.67	2.34	0.26
¾ in.	2.00	2.81	0.31
⅞ in.	2.33	3.28	0.36
1 in.	2.67	3.75	0.42
1⅛ in.	3.00	4.22	—
1¼ in.	3.33	4.69	—
1⅜ in.	3.67	5.16	—
1½ in.	4.00	5.63	—

This formula gives the average thickness, in inches, of hull planking for a wooden boat:

Add the square root of the boat's overall length in feet to her beam in feet, and divide the result by 16. That is:

$$\sqrt{LOA} + \text{beam (in feet)} \div 16 = \text{planking thickness (in inches)}.$$

Example:

1. Boat length overall is 31 feet.

2. Beam is 10 feet 1 inch.

3. Planking thickness $= \sqrt{31} = 5.57 + 10.08 = 15.65 \div 16 = 0.98$ inch.

4. Round up to 1 inch.

Deck planking is usually 80 to 85 percent of the thickness of the hull planking, except that plywood decking may be 75 percent of the thickness.

SCANTLINGS FOR FRAMES, KEEL, AND STEM

Here are average dimensions for wooden boat construction:

Frames	Spacing:	Boat length overall ÷ 34
	Molding (thickness athwartships):	Plank thickness × 1.5
	Siding (thickness fore and aft):	Molding × 1.33
Keel and Stem	Cross-section area:	Plank thickness squared × 12.5

MOISTURE CONTENT OF WOOD

At fiber saturation point, wood contains about 25 percent of moisture by weight.

Air drying will get that down to about 17 percent.

Kiln drying will get it down to 8 percent.

For most boat work, the moisture content of timber should be between 12 and 16 percent.

How to Establish Moisture Content

1. Weigh a small sample of the wood on a sensitive kitchen scale or a postal scale, and note the weight.

2. Dry the sample in a domestic oven at 200°F (95°C), weighing it periodically. When the weight becomes constant, all the moisture has been removed. Note the weight.

3. Divide the weight lost by the original weight of the wet wood. Multiply the result by 100 for the percentage of original moisture content.

Example:

1. Sample of wood before oven drying weighs 4 ounces (114 g).

2. Weight becomes constant at 3 ounces (86 g). Weight loss = 1 ounce (28 g).

3. Weight lost (U.S.) 1 ounce ÷ 4 ounces (original weight) $= 1 ÷ 4 × 100 = 25$ percent moisture content.

   Weight lost (metric) 28 g ÷ 114 g (original weight) $= 28 ÷ 114 × 100 = 25$ percent moisture content.

WOOD DECAY

 To prevent rot, wood must be always wet or always dry. Constantly wet wood resists rot because there is no air present. Constantly dry wood resists rot because there is no moisture present.

Wood rot is the action of fungi feeding on the cellulose between the cell walls. Most fungi flourish only when both fresh water and stagnant air are present. The moisture content of the wood must be about 25 or 30 percent, and the ideal temperature is between 75 and 90°F (24°–32°C).

Some woods have more natural resistance to decay than others. Builders commonly use copper naphthenate (Cuprinol and Woodlife) as a rot preventative. Rock salt strewn inside the hull was traditionally used in wooden fishing boats. Salt water and sunshine also help prevent fungal rot.

CHARACTERISTICS OF PLYWOOD

Exterior-grade plywood and marine-grade plywood both are laminated with waterproof resorcinol glue. The difference is in the quality of the veneers, the number of inner plies, and the gaps, if any, in the core material.

Most U.S. plywood is made from Douglas fir or western larch.

Each face of a plywood panel is graded according to its quality and appearance with a letter of the alphabet; the highest grade is A.

Marine-grade plywood is normally rated A-A (having two excellent sides) or A-B or A-C (having one excellent side and one of lesser quality, for work where one side will not show).

Marine plywood imported from Europe is of high-quality hardwood, usually mahogany or lightweight okoume, laminated to metric thicknesses.

Beam Spacing for Plywood Decks

Plywood Thickness		Beam Spacing	
Inches	mm	Inches	mm
1/4	6	5 3/4	140
3/8	10	8	200
1/2	12	10	225
5/8	16	12	300
3/4	20	14	360

Maximum Bends for Marine Ply

The following table gives the tightest radius to which marine plywood can safely be bent. Moisture content is taken to be about 10 percent. Wetter wood will take a slightly sharper bend.

Plywood Thickness		Radius of Bend along the Grain		Radius of Bend across the Grain	
Inches	mm	Inches	mm	Inches	mm
5/32	4	15	380	9	230
3/16	5	18	455	12	305
1/4	6	24	610	20	510
5/16	8	30	760	30	760
3/8	9	39	990	39	990
1/2	12	60	1,520	45	1,140

Fasteners

TERMINOLOGY

Here are the commonly used terms for the fasteners most often found in boats.

Bolts

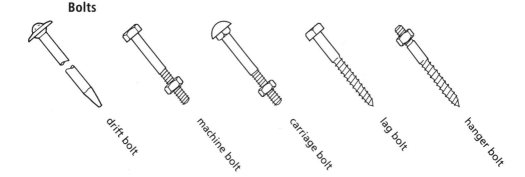

drift bolt   machine bolt   carriage bolt   lag bolt   hanger bolt

Drift bolts. Very long, unthreaded rods driven through timbers to lock them together.

Screw bolts. Common machine bolts, with square or hexagonal heads, used with nuts.

Carriage bolts. Screw bolts with a square neck beneath a mushroom head. The neck stops the shank from turning in the wood when the nut is tightened. Some have flat heads and fins to prevent turning.

Lag bolts. Also called lag screws. Large wood screws with square heads. They are tightened with a wrench.

Hanger bolts. Lag bolts with the head end threaded to take a nut. Fittings may be released without disturbing the bolt in the wood by backing off the nut.

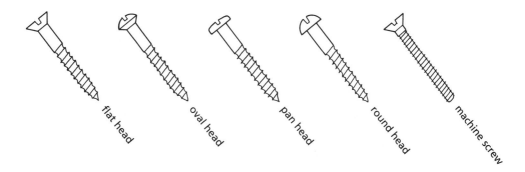

flat head   oval head   pan head   round head   machine screw

Screws

Flat-head screws. Flat topped, with countersunk shafts. Extensively used in woodwork.

Oval-head screws. They have mushroom heads with countersunk shafts. They are usually fitted with cup-shaped finishing washers. Used in light work where fastenings show.

Pan-head screws. The heads are flat (or slightly mushroomed) on top, and flat underneath. Designed for metal work, they find many uses on fiberglass boats.

Round-head screws. The domed heads are flat underneath. Used to fasten thin metal or fiberglass to wood.

Machine screws. Actually small machine bolts, but threaded the entire length of the shank. They have flat, round, or oval heads and come in sizes up to $1/4$ inch (6 mm) shank diameter. Used as through-fasteners for light stuff.

Note: Most screws have either slotted heads or Phillips heads. Many builders use Phillips-head screws to reduce screwdriver slippage and damage to adjacent wood.

Wood screws normally have tapered shafts. Metalwork screws have a short section of taper near the point, but the shafts are otherwise parallel. They are also known as self-tapping screws, that is, they will tap their own thread in fiberglass, or in a thin piece of metal such as an aluminum mast or boom, drilled with a hole slightly smaller in diameter than the screw thread.

Nails

copper wire — galvanized boat — threaded — copper clout — square-shank boat

Copper wire nails. Ordinary, round-shanked, flat-headed nails.

Galvanized boat nails. Forged with a button head and rectangular shank. May be blunt or chisel-pointed.

Threaded nails. Nails with closely spaced, barbed rings, or annular threads, to keep them secured in wood.

Copper clout nails. Flat headed with square shanks. Often used to clench light lapstrake planking.

Square-shank boat nails. Made of copper, with pyramid heads, for riveting planking to frames in conjunction with roves.

METRIC BOLTS

World cruising boats often face the problem of drilling a clearance hole for a metric bolt. This table gives clearances in inches:

Nominal Bolt Diameter		Clearance Drill
mm	Inches	Inches
M3	.118	1/8 or No. 31
M3.5	.138	9/64 or No. 28
M5	.197	13/64 or No. 8
M6	.236	1/4
M8	.315	21/64
M10	.394	13/32
M12	.472	31/64
M14	.551	9/16

AVAILABILITY OF STANDARD BOLT LENGTHS AND DIAMETERS

Length		Diameter				
Inches	mm	1/4 in. 6 mm	5/16 in. 8 mm	3/8 in. 10 mm	1/2 in. 12 mm	5/8 in. 16 mm
3/8	10	✓	—	—	—	—
1/2	12	✓	✓	—	—	—
5/8	16	✓	✓	✓	—	—
3/4	20	✓	✓	✓	✓	—
1	25	✓	✓	✓	✓	✓
1 1/4	30	✓	✓	✓	✓	✓
	35	✓	✓	✓	✓	✓
1 1/2	40	✓	✓	✓	✓	✓
1 3/4	45	✓	✓	✓	✓	✓
2	50	✓	✓	✓	✓	✓
2 1/4	55	✓	✓	✓	✓	✓
	60	✓	✓	✓	✓	✓
2 1/2	65	✓	✓	✓	✓	✓
	70	✓	✓	✓	✓	✓
3	75	✓	✓	✓	✓	✓
	80	✓	✓	✓	✓	✓
3 1/2	90	—	✓	✓	✓	✓
4	100	—	✓	✓	✓	✓
	110	—	—	✓	✓	✓
4 1/2	120	—	—	✓	✓	✓
5	130	—	—	—	✓	✓
	140	—	—	—	✓	✓
6	150	—	—	—	✓	✓

✓ Commonly available   — Not off-the-shelf

PILOT HOLE SIZES FOR WOOD SCREWS

Make the lead hole size 90 percent of the diameter of the screw at the beginning of the threads for hardwood, and 70 percent for softwood.

BOLT STRENGTH

Bolts of bronze or steel have a tensile strength of roughly 60,000 pounds per square inch of section area (4,219 kg/cm²).

High-tensile bolts are about twice as strong as ordinary bolts.

Brass bolts have only 20 to 33 percent of the strength of ordinary bronze or steel bolts.

KEEL BOLT STRENGTH

Keel bolts of galvanized mild steel or bronze, with a tensile strength of not less than 60,000 pounds per square inch (4,219 kg/cm²), should have a cross-sectional area of a minimum of 1 square inch (6.452 square centimeters) for every 1,500 pounds (680 kg) of keel weight.

Monel or stainless steel bolts, which have a tensile strength of 80,000 pounds per square inch (5,625 kg/cm²) or more, may be proportionately smaller.

SCREWS FOR WOODEN PLANKING

These are the sizes of screws traditionally used for fastening wooden planking. Screws used for decking should be the same length as shown here but may be one gauge thinner. Screws smaller than 5/8 in. #9 are usually puttied over but may be finished with wooden plugs for varnished planking.

Planking Thickness	Length and Gauge	Screw Diameter	Body Drill	Lead Drill	Plug Diameter
1/8 in.	1/2 in. #6	0.137 in.	1/8 in.	#47	—
3/8 in.	3/4 in. #7	0.150 in.	9/64 in.	#44	—
1/2 in.	1 in. #8	0.163 in.	5/32 in.	#40	—
5/8 in.	1 1/4 in. #9	0.176 in.	11/64 in.	#37	3/8 in.
3/4 in.	1 1/2 in. #10	0.189 in.	3/16 in.	#33	1/2 in.
7/8 in.	1 3/4 in. #12	0.216 in.	13/64 in.	#30	1/2 in.
1 in.	2 in. #14	0.242 in.	15/64 in.	#25	1/2 in.
1 1/8 in.	2 1/4 in. #16	0.268 in.	17/64 in.	#18	5/8 in.
1 1/4 in.	2 1/2 in. #18	0.294 in.	9/32 in.	#13	5/8 in.
1 1/2 in.	3 in. #20	0.320 in.	5/16 in.	#4	3/4 in.

Boatbuilding Metals

Dissimilar metals in an electrolyte such as seawater will form an electric cell when connected by a conductor. Electrolytic corrosion eats away the anode, the active electrode, which comprises the less noble metal. The farther apart two metals are on this list, the greater the rate of corrosion of the less noble one of the pair.

BOATBUILDING METALS

Least Noble → **Anodic (active)**

Magnesium and its alloys
Zinc
Galvanized steel
Galvanized wrought iron
Aluminum alloys
Cadmium
Mild steel
Wrought iron
Cast iron
Ni-Resist
Stainless steel, 13 percent chromium, type 410 (active in still water)
Lead tin solder (50-50)
Stainless steel, 18-8, type 304
Stainless steel, type 316 (active)
Lead
Monel (70 percent Cu, 30 percent Ni)
Tin
Muntz metal (60 percent Cu, 40 percent Zn)
Manganese bronze (58.5 percent Cu, 39 percent Zn, 1 percent Sn, 1 percent Fe, 0.3 percent Mn)
Naval brass (60 percent Cu, 39 percent Zn)
Nickel (active)
Yellow brass (65 percent Cu, 35 percent Zn)
Aluminum bronze (92 percent Cu, 8 percent Al)
Red brass (85 percent Cu, 15 percent Zn)
Copper
Admiralty Brass (71 percent Cu, 28 percent Zn, 1 percent Sn)
Aluminum brass (76 percent Cu, 22 percent Zn, 2 percent Al)
Silicon bronze (93 percent Cu, 0.8 percent Fe, 1.5 percent Zn, 2 percent Si, 0.75 percent Mn, 1.6 percent Sn)
Bronze, Composition G (88 percent Cu, 2 percent Zn, 10 percent Sn)
Bronze, Composition M (88 percent Cu, 3 percent Zn, 6.5 percent Sn, 1.5 percent Pb)
Nickel (passive)
Stainless steel, 13 percent chromium, type 410 (passive)
Stainless steel, 18-8, type 304 (passive)
Stainless steel, type 316 (passive)
Hastelloy C
Titanium
Platinum

Most Noble → **Cathodic (passive)**

ALUMINUM ROD: WEIGHT IN POUNDS PER FOOT

Diameter, or Width Across Flats

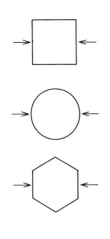

Inches	mm	Round	Hexagonal	Square
1/8 in.	3 mm	.014	.016	.018
3/16 in.	4.8 mm	.032	.036	.041
1/4 in.	6.4 mm	.058	.064	.074
5/16 in.	8 mm	.090	.099	.115
3/8 in.	9.5 mm	.130	.143	.165
7/16 in.	11 mm	.177	.195	.225
1/2 in.	12.7 mm	.231	.255	.294
9/16 in.	14 mm	.292	.322	.372
5/8 in.	16 mm	.361	.398	.415
11/16 in.	17.5 mm	.437	.481	.507
3/4 in.	19 mm	.520	.573	.608
13/16 in.	20.6 mm	.610	.672	.718
7/8 in.	22.2 mm	.707	.779	.837
15/16 in.	23.8 mm	.812	.895	.966
1 in.	25.4 mm	.924	1.018	1.104

Note: Multiply pounds per foot by 1.488 to convert to kilograms per meter.

BRASS AND STEEL ROD

Brass weighs about 535 pounds per cubic foot (796 kg/m³), and ordinary steel about 490 pounds per cubic foot (729 kg/m³). Stainless steel weighs approximately 500 pounds per cubic foot (744 kg/m³). But for most practical purposes, the following table will serve for estimating the weight of both brass and steel rod.

Diameter, or Width Across Flats — **Weight in Pounds per Foot**

Inches	mm	Round	Hexagonal	Square
1/8 in.	3 mm	.0450	.0497	.0574
3/16 in.	4.8 mm	.1014	.1118	.1291
1/4 in.	6.4 mm	.1803	.1988	.2295
5/16 in.	8 mm	.2817	.3106	.3586
3/8 in.	9.5 mm	.4055	.4472	.5164
7/16 in.	11 mm	.5520	.6087	.7029
1/2 in.	12.7 mm	.7210	.7950	.9180
9/16 in.	14 mm	.9125	1.0062	1.1619
5/8 in.	16 mm	1.1265	1.2422	1.4344
11/16 in.	17.5 mm	1.3632	1.5031	1.7356
3/4 in.	19 mm	1.6223	1.7888	2.0655
13/16 in.	20.6 mm	1.9039	2.0993	2.4241
7/8 in.	22.2 mm	2.2080	2.4347	2.8114
15/16 in.	23.8 mm	2.5348	2.7949	3.2274
1 in.	25.4 mm	2.8840	3.1800	3.6720

Note: Multiply pounds per foot by 1.488 to convert to kilograms per meter.

As already mentioned, steel is lighter than brass by about 8 percent, but for most practical purposes, the following table will suffice for both.

Gauge Number	Diameter (Inches)	Lb. per 100 feet	Gauge Number	Diameter (Inches)	Lb. per 100 feet
7/0	.500	72.34	13	.092	2.45
6/0	.464	62.30	15	.072	1.50
5/0	.432	54.00	17	.056	0.908
4/0	.400	46.29	19	.040	0.464
3/0	.373	40.04	21	.032	0.297
2/0	.348	35.04	23	.024	0.167
0	.324	30.38	25	.020	0.116
1	.300	26.04	27	.0164	0.0779
3	.252	18.37	29	.0136	0.0536
5	.212	13.00	31	.0116	0.0389
7	.176	8.96	33	.0100	0.0290
9	.144	6.00	36	.0076	0.0167
11	.116	3.89			

BOATBUILDING METALS

The weight of other gauges may be estimated by simple interpolation. Multiply pounds per 100 feet by 1.488 to convert to kilograms per 100 meters.

WEIGHTS OF METALS

These are the weights, in pounds per cubic foot, of metals commonly found on sailboats:

Aluminum	166	Iron, cast	450
Aluminum bronze	480	Lead	710
Brass	535	Steel	490
Bronze	525	Stainless steel	500
Copper	556		

Note: Multiply pounds per cubic foot by 16.02 to convert to kilograms per cubic meter.

COMPOSITION OF COMMON BOATBUILDING METALS

The composition of many alloys varies within certain limits. This table lists the typical percentages of elements found in the alloys most commonly available.

Al = aluminum; Cu = copper; Fe = iron; Mn = manganese; Ni = nickel; Pb = lead; Si = Silicon; Sn = tin; Zn = zinc.

Brass, Admiralty	Cu 71, Zn 28, Sn 1
Brass, aluminum	Cu 76, Zn 22, Al 2
Brass, yellow	Cu 65, Zn 35
Bronze, aluminum	Cu 92, Al 8
Bronze, Composition M	Cu 88, Zn 3, Sn 6.5, Pb 1.5
Bronze, Composition G	Cu 88, Zn 2, Sn 10
Bronze, manganese	Cu 58.5, Zn 39, Sn 1, Fe 1, Mn 0.3
Bronze, silicon	Cu 93, Fe 0.8, Zn 1.5, Si 2, Mn 0.75, Sn 1.6
Bronze, Tobin	Cu 60, Zn 39
Cupro-nickel	Cu 90, Ni 10
Gunmetal	Cu 88, Sn 12
Monel	Cu 70, Ni 30
Muntz metal	Cu 60, Zn 40

STAINLESS STEEL RIGGING WIRE

The stainless steel commonly used for standing rigging wire is type 302/304, the commercial grade.

Type 316 stainless steel wire rope—with 18 percent chromium, 8 percent nickel, and 3 percent molybdenum—is more resistant to corrosion, though, and is strongly recommended for tropical marine use.

But type 316 is about 15 percent weaker than type 302/304, so rigging wire sizes must be upgraded accordingly.

For the strengths of stainless steel wires, see "Sails, Spars, and Rigging."

The Galley

ESSENTIAL COOKING AND EATING EQUIPMENT

This basic list of galley hardware caters to a cruising crew of four. It is also a helpful reminder for racing crews, although they will no doubt lighten ship by leaving ashore such fancy items as dessert spoons and table knives.

1 Frying pan or skillet with lid
2 Large saucepans with lids
1 Small saucepan
1 Kettle
1 Chopping board
1 Cook's knife, large
1 Cook's knife, small
1 Vegetable peeler
2 Can openers
1 Corkscrew
1 Hole-punch for cans
1 Spatula
1 Wooden spoon
2 Tablespoons
4 Dessert spoons
4 Teaspoons
4 Table knives
4 Forks

4 Mugs or cups
4 Glasses
4 Soup/cereal bowls
6 Plates
1 Plastic or stainless steel mixing bowl
1 Measuring cup
1 Set measuring spoons
2 Large vacuum flasks
1 Wire whisk
3 Small plastic containers with lids
  (for leftovers)
1 Washing-up bowl, if necessary
1 Plastic bucket
1 Garbage pail
1 Colander
Salt and pepper shakers
Toothpicks
Paper towels
Dishcloths or sponges
Dish towels
Aluminum foil
Freezer bags
Matches

IDEAL GALLEY DIMENSIONS

A Worktop height for standing person: 2 feet 9½ inches (850 mm)

B Worktop width: 2 feet (600 mm)

C Shelf height above worktop: minimum 1 foot 4 inches (400 mm)

D Width of shelves over worktop: maximum 12 inches (300 mm)

E Kick space under galley cupboards at sole level: 3 inches × 3 inches (75 mm × 75 mm)

F Maximum reach to back of lockers over worktop: 2 feet 6 inches (750 mm)

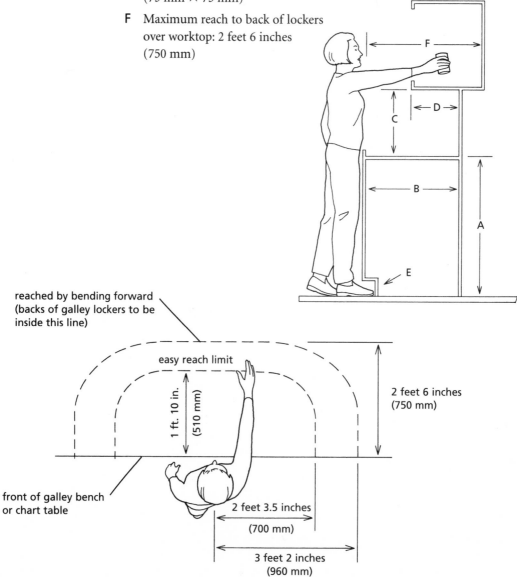

reached by bending forward (backs of galley lockers to be inside this line)

easy reach limit

1 ft. 10 in. (510 mm)

2 feet 6 inches (750 mm)

front of galley bench or chart table

2 feet 3.5 inches (700 mm)

3 feet 2 inches (960 mm)

OVEN TEMPERATURES

Rating	Degrees F	Degrees C
Warming	200–250	90–120
Slow cooking	250–300	120–150
Slow to moderate	300–350	150–180
Moderate	350–375	180–200
Moderate to hot	375–425	200–220
Hot	425–450	220–230
Very hot	450–500	230–260

COOKING FUELS COMPARED

Fuel	Btu per Gallon	Approximate Cost per Hour	Hours per Gallon
Alcohol	64,600	$0.21	32
Kerosene (Paraffin)	129,350	$0.07	32
LPG (Butane or Propane)	91,000	$0.10	17

CROCKERY AND GLASSWARE

Item	Diameter	Height	Height of Two Stacked
Large plate	$10^{1/2}$ in. (270 mm)	$^{13}/_{16}$ in. (20 mm)	$1^{1/8}$ in. (28 mm)
Soup plate	8 in. (205 mm)	$1^{3}/_{16}$ in. (30 mm)	$1^{7}/_{16}$ in. (36 mm)
Side plate	7 in. (180 mm)	$^{5/8}$ in. (16 mm)	$^{15}/_{16}$ in. (24 mm)
Saucer	$6^{5/8}$ in. (170 mm)	$1^{3}/_{16}$ in. (30 mm)	$1^{1/2}$ in. (38 mm)
Cup	$3^{1/2}$ in. (90 mm)	$2^{7/8}$ in. (73 mm)	
Mug	$3^{1/2}$ in. (90 mm)	4 in. (100 mm)	
Tumbler	3 in. (75 mm)	$5^{1/2}$ in. (140 mm)	

Food and Water

FRESH WATER

 For drinking only, about half a gallon (2 liters) per person per day is adequate to maintain good health if it's supplemented by soft drinks and canned juices. A gallon (3.78 liters) a day is preferable as a minimum in hot climates, especially if it's the only potable liquid.

Good water will remain sweet for at least six months in tightly sealed opaque containers stored in a cool place away from bright light.

 A human being can survive:

1. Three minutes without air
2. Three days without water
3. Three weeks without food

WATER PURIFICATION

Sometimes there is no option but to take on water from less-than-desirable sources.

To sterilize 15 gallons (60 liters) of fresh water, add one teaspoonful (5 ml) of 5.25 percent household bleach, such as Clorox.

The active ingredient, sodium hypochlorite, is toxic to humans as well as to germs, but does its job swiftly and then breaks down about 10 minutes after being exposed to light and air. Leave the filler tap off the tank for 30 minutes to an hour to be sure the toxic chlorine gas has dissipated into the surrounding air. Be cautious when first tasting the purified water—an excess of chlorine will burn your mouth and throat.

A good way to test for safety is to put some water in a glass and place your palm over the top. Shake the glass, and then smell your wet palm. It should smell no more of chlorine than does the usual city water from a household faucet.

To clean and flush a water tank, add a cupful (250 ml) of 5.25 percent liquid bleach to every 50 gallons (200 liters) of water. After 10 minutes, pump the water through all your faucets and pipes. Then drain the tank and refill it with fresh water.

Chlorine eventually attacks stainless steel, so allow the bleach to break down by exposing the water's surface to fresh air for at least 10 minutes before sealing the tank.

Note: Never add bleach to a water tank connected to a reverse-osmosis water maker—the bleach will damage it.

SHELF LIFE OF GALLEY STORES

Shelf Life	Item
Three months	Vegetable oils
Four months	Ready-to-eat cereals, sealed
	Sugar, brown or powdered
Six months	Milk, evaporated, and nonfat dry or whole milk in a metal container
	Pancake mix in an airtight container
	Rice
	Instant breakfasts in original packaging
Nine months	Peanut butter, sealed
One year	Baking soda and powder
	Bouillon products
	Cereals, uncooked, in paper
	Cream, instant dry
	Flour in an airtight container
	Honey, jam, syrup
	Hydrogenated solid shortening
	Pudding mixes, unopened
Eighteen months	Cocoa, coffee, and tea, instant
	Hard candy, gum
	Potatoes, instant
Two years	Sugar, granulated
	Cool drink, powdered
	Salt

Canned food gradually changes in flavor, texture, color, and aroma, but will normally be fit to eat for at least the periods listed below. If possible, stored canned goods should be used in rotation well before these periods are up. All canned food should be stored in a cool, dry place.

Golden rule: Throw out cans that are bulging, rusting, or damaged—their contents can be deadly.

Shelf Life	Item
One year	Milk products (including evaporated milk, cream, and milk puddings)
	Prunes
	Rhubarb
	Nuts
	Fish
	Berries and sour cherries
	Citrus fruit juice
	Dried fruit
	Tomatoes
	Sauerkraut
	Cereals
	Hydrogenated solid shortening
Eighteen months	Blackberries, gooseberries, plums, black currants, raspberries, and strawberries
	New potatoes
	Poultry
	Dry beans and dry peas
	Coffee, tea, cocoa
Two years	Vegetables (except new potatoes)
	Baked beans
	Pasta products
	Soups
	Ready meals
	Hot meat products
	Rice
Five years	Solid-pack meat products
	Fish in oil

FOOD & WATER

Shelf Life	Item
2 to 3 weeks	Ice cream
1 month	Cooked fish
2 to 3 months	Cooked meat
	Bread, with preservatives
3 months	Cooked meat pies, stews, casseroles, meat salads
3 to 4 months	Fresh liver, heart, kidney
	Fresh ground meat, stew meat
3 to 6 months	Fresh roasts, steaks, chops
	Fresh fish
6 months	Cooked poultry, cooked poultry pies, stews, gravies
6 to 8 months	Fresh poultry

AVERAGE FOOD CONSUMPTION

For cruise-planning purposes, it's useful to figure that food for the average crewmember will weigh 5 to 6 pounds (2.5 kg) a day, including the packaging.

Average serving size of some common foods is as follows:

Bread	6 to 8 ounces (200 g)
Cheese	4 ounces (100 g)
Fish	6 to 8 ounces (200 g)
Fresh fruit	6 ounces (150 g)
Fresh meat	6 to 8 ounces (200 g)
Fresh vegetables	8 ounces (250 g)

Average weekly consumption per person:

Butter	8 ounces (250 g)
Canned desserts	two 16-ounce (450-g) cans
Canned vegetables	one 16-ounce (450-g) can
Coffee, ground	4 ounces (125 g)
Coffee, instant	1.75 ounces (50 g)
Cocoa	3.5 ounces (100 g)
Eggs	6
Fresh milk	4 pints (2 liters)
Jam	8 ounces (250 g)
Oil	1 pint (500 ml)
Pasta	8 ounces (250 g)
Potatoes	4 pounds (2 kg)
Rice	1 pound (450 g)
Sugar, granulated	8 ounces (250 g)
Tea	10 tea bags

FOOD & WATER

Merely to sustain life in an emergency, you need (per person, per day) about ⅔ pint (315 ml) of fresh water and 600 calories (2,500 kilojoules) of food—say 5 to 6 ounces (140 to 170 g) of hard candy, sugar, or fatty cookies.

SOURCES OF VITAMIN C

Scurvy, the plague of seafarers in olden times, is caused by a deficiency of vitamin C. Scurvy is easier to get than you might imagine, especially on long, tropical ocean crossings on boats without refrigeration.

Symptoms: Scurvy patients suffer a general feeling of weakness. Flesh on the legs may become flabby and erupt with sores. Scurvy also causes spongy, bleeding gums, and bleeding from mucous membranes.

Prevention: By law, U.S. vessels were required to provide "lime or lemon juice and sugar daily, at the rate of half-a-pint per week for each member of the crew."

Fresh fruit, vegetables, and most of the constituents of salads also are valuable sources of vitamin C. Potatoes, especially when cooked in their skins, are particularly good.

And, of course, vitamin C is widely available in capsule and tablet form.

FOOD & WATER

Paints

According to the old rule, a gallon of enamel paint or varnish would cover 500 square feet. One liter would cover about 12 square meters.

By the same old rule, one gallon of antifouling bottom paint would cover 350 to 400 square feet, and one liter would cover 8.5 to 9.5 square meters.

But modern paint finishes vary so greatly in their covering capacity you'll need to refer to the manufacturers' cans or brochures for the amount of paint required to cover a certain area.

Here's how to estimate the area to be painted. Measurements in feet give results in square feet. Measurements in meters give results in square meters:

Topsides area (both sides) = (length overall + beam) × 2 × average freeboard.

Area of bottom of hull (to waterline) = load waterline × beam × draft. For full-keel cruising boats, use 75 percent of the result. For light-displacement boats, use 50 percent of the result.

Deck area = length overall × beam × 0.75. Subtract area of cockpit and deck structures.

Spar area = length overall × 2.5 × average diameter.

BOTTOM PAINT TYPES

Ablative Ablative, or copolymer, antifouling paint gradually and constantly wears away to reveal a new surface of copper biocide. It wears both from chemical reaction with water, and from the scouring action of water on the hull. As long as paint remains, however, it is always 100 percent effective.

Ablative bottom paint retains its biocidal properties no matter how long it's out of the water. Most ablative coatings are comparatively expensive as they require a minimum of two, and preferably three, coats.

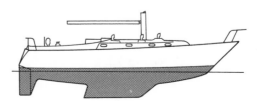

Sloughing (ablative) Sloughing paints also wear away constantly, but they use a softer resin binder than do copolymer paints. While they are cheaper than other ablative types, sloughing paints lose their effectiveness very quickly if they are exposed to air.

Modified Epoxy (non-ablative) Modified epoxy antifouling paints lose only their copper content, not the paint. Copper particles embedded in the epoxy gradually dissolve and allow the water to penetrate deeper and deeper until all the copper biocide is used up. Epoxy may be scrubbed to renew its effectiveness but gradually loses potency out of the water. This is the best choice for boats left in the water year-round.

Vinyl (non-ablative) Vinyl antifouling paint is similar in action to epoxy. It develops a very hard, smooth finish that may be burnished for racing hulls. It does not wear away; it loses effectiveness gradually out of the water. If it is applied over other types of bottom paint, its powerful solvents can cause them to soften and bubble.

Teflon A specialized bottom coating for racing craft. Provides a thin, hard coating. The slippery surface reduces underwater drag and may be burnished, but it has no biocidal properties. Ideal for boats removed from the water after each use. Incompatible with antifouling paints.

BOTTOM PAINT COMPATIBILITY

Old Paint	New Paint			
	Ablative	Epoxy	Sloughing	Vinyl
Ablative	1	1	1	4
Epoxy	1	1	1	4
Sloughing	4	3	1	4
Vinyl	2	2	2	2

KEY
1 Lightly sand old coat.
2 Moderately sand old coat.
3 Heavily sand old coat.
4 Remove all traces of old coat.

CHARACTERISTICS OF TOPSIDE PAINTS

Type of Paint	Ease of Use	Relative Cost	Durability	Solvent	Toxicity
Alkyd enamel	Easy for amateurs. Dries slowly and is very forgiving.	Not cheap, but good value.	Good. Retains color and gloss well.	Mineral spirits.	Relatively low.
Alkyd-Silicone enamel	Same as alkyd.	Slightly more than alkyd.	Better gloss retention than alkyd.	Mineral spirits.	Relatively low.
Alkyd-Acrylic enamel	Same as alkyd.	Slightly more than alkyd.	Gloss and color retention slightly better than alkyd.	Mineral spirits.	Relatively low.
Polyurethane (single-pack), oil-modified	As easy as alkyd, but dries faster.	More expensive than alkyd.	Longer lasting and better scuff resistance than alkyd.	Mineral spirits.	Relatively low.
Polyurethane (twin-pack), linear	Moderately difficult, but gets easier with practice.	Very expensive, but good value for money.	Very durable Highly resistant to stains, impact, and scratches.	Aromatics, esters, and ketones.	Low when brushed or rolled. Very high when sprayed.
Epoxy	Trickier than alkyd. Dries fast.	Between alkyd and polyurethane.	Normally used as primer and undercoat only.	Similar to twin-pack polyurethane.	Use with care. Don't breathe fumes.

SANDPAPER GRADES

Sandpaper comes in a bewildering array of types and grits. But most boat work can be accomplished with just two kinds of paper and about half-a-dozen grits.

All dry sanding can be done with aluminum oxide production paper. It's backed with brown paper, and the grit is sharp, tough, and long lasting—probably the best for sanding fiberglass.

The grits most commonly needed are 80 for initial rough sanding, 120 for early sanding between coats of paint or for smoothing wood, and 220 for fine sanding between coats.

Wet sanding is done with waterproof silicon carbide, or wet-and-dry paper, which is the color of charcoal. It, too, is sharp and long lasting; keep it wet to prevent clogging. Its main use is sanding between coats of paint or varnish for an extrafine finish, and for this purpose you should use 360- or 400-grit. It's also good for sanding bottom paint without causing dust. Use 40-grit for removing old antifouling paint and 80-grit between coats.

Fillers, Cements, & Fairing Compounds

Preparing a surface for a fine paint or varnish finish involves filling the grain of wood and any scratches or hollow blemishes in fiberglass with material that is easily sanded smooth when it dries or cures.

Fairing Compound

Fairing compounds come in many different types for special jobs. All will fill small dents and holes, some will fill quite deep hollow patches in a hull, and most will cure to a light material that is easily sanded to a feather edge. They are usually finished off with a glazing compound or a surfacing compound before they're painted.

Glazing Compound

Glazing compounds (marine, not household) are applied in thin layers to fill small scratches and mend minor surface damage in readiness for a primer or undercoat.

Sanding Surfacer

Sanding surfacers are thick coats of paint, brushed or sprayed on to seal old, porous gelcoat and to fill crazing or scratches. Some, such as the epoxies, need to be sanded almost completely away to form a perfectly smooth surface for subsequent coats of paint, but care should be taken not to break right through the surfacer.

Seam Compound

Seam compounds fill the seams of wooden-planked and wooden-decked hulls. The compound should adhere to two sides only, to allow sideways expansion and contraction without destroying the seal. Caulking cotton in a seam, incidentally, serves to prevent the compound from sticking to wood on the third side (the bottom), which is often the cause of leaks.

Surfacing Putty

Surfacing putties, like glazing compounds, fill small imperfections before paint is applied, although surfacing putty is capable of hiding holes up to $1/4$ inch (6 mm) deep. They are smoothed on with a flexible putty knife.

Trowel Cement

Trowel cements are heavier-bodied than glazing compounds and are used to fill dents, holes, and gouges in painted surfaces above the waterline. They sand and fair easily. Apply them with a putty knife.

Wood Filler

Wood fillers penetrate the pores of the wood, bringing it up to a level surface. They reduce the number of coats of paint or varnish that would otherwise be needed to build up a smooth surface. And they add color if needed.

Sealants and Glues

Sealants form tough but flexible gaskets between fittings. When used to bed deck hardware, they prevent water from dripping through the fastener holes, and they electrically isolate different metals. In addition, some sealants have great adhesive powers. The three sealants most often used on sailboats are:

Polyurethane Polyurethane, which is used for hull-to-deck joints and other joints that require a permanent bond. Polyurethane is a powerful glue, and should not be used on fittings that will later need to be removed. It bonds well to most boat materials and is used above and below the waterline, but it should not be used with Lexan or ABS plastic. Some polyurethanes cannot be painted.

Polysulfide Polysulfide, which comes in single packs and twin packs. Single-part polysulfides are as durable as the two-part versions but take longer to cure. Polysulfide is used for almost all kinds of sealing and bedding, and will permit the later removal of hardware. Polysulfides bond well to most surfaces except plastic, which they melt. When it's used as seam filler on oily wood, such as teak, the wood must be treated with the recommended primer to remove the oil. Most polysulfides can be painted or varnished.

Silicone Silicone is safe with all materials including plastics. Very tough and elastic, it forms excellent removable gaskets that are highly heat- and chemical-resistant. It does not have the adhesive qualities of polyurethane, but some newer silicones with improved adhesion can be very difficult to remove. Silicone bonds well to fiberglass, glass, metal, plastic, and wood, but will not take paint.

SEALANT/BEDDING TABLE

KEY
1 Excellent
2 Very good
3 Good
4 Not recommended

Materials	Polysulfide	Polyurethane	Silicone
ABS and Lexan plastic to fiberglass	4	4	3
ABS and Lexan plastic to wood	4	4	3
Deck/hull joints	1	1	2
Deck seams	1	4	4
Electrical insulation	2	1	1
Fiberglass to fiberglass	2	1	2
Glass to fiberglass	2	1	2
Glass to metal	2	1	2
Glass to vinyl	4	4	3
Glass to wood	1	2	3
Metal to wood	1	2	3
Metal to fiberglass	1	1	2
Planking seams (underwater)	1	4	4
Plastic to fiberglass	4	4	2
Plastic to wood	4	4	3
Wood to fiberglass	1	1	2
Wood to wood	1	1	2

SEALANTS

79

Most glues used in boat work fall into one of four categories:

Rubber   Rubber, natural and synthetic. This includes contact adhesives.

Melamine-urea Types   These are water-resistant glues suitable for amateur use, including Weldwood plastic resin glue, Casco urea-formaldehyde, and Aerolite resin glues.

Epoxies   Well-known epoxy resin in its many forms is excellent for most marine work, including laminating new fiberglass to GRP hulls. It fills gaps and forms an effective sealer coat. But most epoxy is rated water resistant, not waterproof, and may be adversely affected by salt water and sunlight.

Resorcinols   The best wood-to-wood glue available for marine use, resorcinol is fully waterproof and not affected by sunlight. It comes in two forms: one needs temperatures of 70 degrees F (21 degrees C) or higher to cure; the other, an imported version made by Ciba-Geigy (Aerodux or Cascophen) will cure in temperatures as low as 50 degrees F (10 degrees C). It is not gap-filling, however. The U.S. product is made by Weldwood and is available at marine hardware stores.

Some modern bedding compounds are almost as adhesive as glue and might be considered glues in their own right. In particular, polyurethane sealants form strong, long-lasting adhesives with gap-filling ability. They do not require firm clamping and are easier to clean up than epoxy.

Note: Plastic materials commonly used on boats fall into one of two groups: thermosetting plastics such as polyester resin, Formica, and melamine; and thermoplastics such as polyvinyl chloride (PVC), acrylic glass substitutes, nylon, polyethylene, and polypropylene.

When heated, thermoplastics soften and melt. Thermosetting plastics do not. They become permanently hard and unmoldable after their initial exposure to heat.

Some glues, sealants, and bedding compounds will melt certain plastics. Always read the manufacturers' fine print.

SEALANTS

	Metal	Fabric	Rubber	Wood	Paper	Ceramic	Thermo-plastic set	Thermo-plastic material
Metal	2,3	1	1,2,3	1,3	1	2,3	1,2,3	1
Fabric	1	1	1	1	1	1	1	1
Rubber	1,2,3	1	1,2,3	1,2	1	1,2	1	1
Wood	1,3	1	1,2	2,3,4	1	1,2	1,2,3	1
Paper	1	1	1	1	1	1	1	1
Ceramic	2,3	1	1,2	1,2	1	2,3	1,2,3	1
Thermosetting plastic	1,2,3	1	1	1,2,3	1	1,2,3	1,2,3	1,2
Thermoplastic materials	1	1	1	1	1	1	1,2	1,2

KEY

1	Rubber or synthetic-rubber glues
2	Melamine-urea glues
3	Epoxy resins
4	Resorcinols

SEALANTS

Plumbing

Rule No. 1:   Every hole in the hull below the waterline must be backed by a seacock.

Rule No. 2:   A gate valve should not be used as a seacock.

Special through-hull fittings of bronze or plastic should line every underwater hole in the hull. Seacocks are either attached directly to the through-hull fitting, or may be an integral part of the through-hull fitting with flanges for bolting them to the hull. There are three basic varieties for marine use:

* the traditional tapered plug seacock

* the T-bar type with a swelling plug

* the ball-valve type

Each has its pros and cons:

Tapered Plug Seacocks

Tapered plug seacocks made of bronze must be dismantled and serviced at least once a year. If they are used a lot, they displace the grease inside and tend to weep constantly. If they are not used a lot, they tend to seize up. Nevertheless, this is a safe design that will rarely spring any nasty surprises. It is still widely used and highly recommended.

T-bar Seacocks

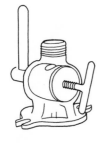

T-bar seacocks have bodies of bronze like the tapered plug seacocks. But instead of tapered bronze plug, a T-bar saecock has a cylindrical neoprene plug. A threaded T-bar shortens the plug when it is turned, and forces it to swell in the middle, making a very efficient seal. T-bar seacocks should not be fitted to through-hulls handling discharge from the galley or the head, however, because it is possible for chemicals to make neoprene swell and prevent the seacock from opening or closing.

Ball-Valve Seacocks

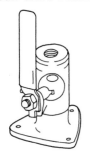

Ball-valve seacocks have a hole running through the middle of a chrome-plated bronze or stainless steel ball turning in Teflon seals. With bronze bodies, they are almost maintenance free (a smear of Vaseline once a year) and never seem to freeze. Ball-valve seacocks made of Marelon, a glass-reinforced nylon, have gained wide acceptance, and in addition to the merits of the bronze-bodied ball-valve types, they are completely corrosion free. They will melt in a fire, however.

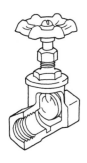

Gate valves are often fitted by manufacturers in place of proper seacocks because they are cheap. But they have no place on a boat. The brass of which they're usually made corrodes quickly in salt water, and there is no visible indication of whether they're properly closed, or whether the gate has clamped down on a piece of debris, leaving a wide gap. Because they usually lack a mounting flange, they are flimsier than seacocks and consequently are not recommended for marine use.

Seacocks and through-hull fittings for pleasure boats are available in a wide range of sizes up to about 3 inches (75 mm) interior diameter, but note carefully that no dimension on what is called a 1½-inch through-hull fitting actually measures 1½ inches. Seacocks, through-hulls, hoses, piping, and connecting fittings should all be bought at the same time and checked for compatibility.

Minimum Interior Diameter (ID) for Seacocks, Through-Hulls, and Hoses

Boat LOA	Toilet Inlet	Toilet Discharge	Basins and Sinks
to 50 feet to 15 m	¾ in. 20 mm	1½ in. 38 mm	¾ – 1½ in. 20–38 mm
over 50 feet over 15 m	1 in. 25 mm	2 in. 50 mm	1¼ –1½ in. 32– 38 mm

Minimum Galley Drain Size

 Small drain pipes for galley sinks should be avoided because they block easily. A ¾-inch (20 mm) ID pipe is the absolute minimum.

Most plumbing on small boats is done with flexible hoses. Because almost everything moves in relationship to everything else, even if only slightly (the engine, the cockpit floor, the decks, the hull), there is little call for the kind of rigid piping found ashore.

Three kinds of hoses (two commonly used on automobiles) deal with the vast majority of boat plumbing jobs:

Auto Heater Hose Silicone rubber heater hose, designed to handle high temperatures, is usually chosen for exhaust hoses handling engine-cooling water. Internal reinforcement of wire or woven material keeps the hose from expanding under pressure and hot working conditions.

Auto Radiator Hose Usually 1½ inches (38 mm) in diameter, radiator hose has a stiff wire reinforcement, so it does not collapse under suction. It's used on boats for bilge pumps, engine raw-water intake lines, toilet intake lines, and cockpit drains.

PVC Tubing For freshwater systems, clear PVC should be FDA-approved as nontoxic. Clear PVC with nylon reinforcing is available for hot or cold pressure-water systems.

For lines supplying salt water to the galley or to the head, an opaque, light-tight variety should be used to discourage the growth of marine organisms.

PVC hose on the discharge side of bilge pumps allows you to check on the flow of water.

Nonpermeable sanitation hose is available for the discharge side of the head.

Special Hoses Special hoses are needed for gas, oil, fuel filler, and refrigeration lines. Get expert professional advice when they need replacing.

Checking Old Hoses The way to check the condition of old hoses is to squeeze them. The material should feel firm, and bounce back when you let go. The hose should be replaced immediately if it

- is hard and brittle
- is soft and spongy
- has splits or cracks
- is kinked, collapsed, or flattened.

Hose Clamps Hoses attached to seacocks and through-hull fittings must be clamped with two stainless steel hose clamps at each end—that is, four clamps per hose.

TANKS

Materials for Tanks

Material	Liquid	Pros	Cons	Notes
Aluminum alloys	Fresh water and fuels	Light, and resists oxidation	Vulnerable to electrolytic corrosion	Expensive to fabricate specially
Fiberglass	Fresh water, sewage, or fuel	May be built into difficult spaces	Should be coated inside against osmosis	Can be made of plywood covered with fiberglass
Monel	Fresh water, sewage, or fuel	Long lasting, most resistant to corrosion	Very expensive	No painting needed, inside or out
Plastic, rigid	Fresh water, sewage, or fuel	Cheap, ready-made, off-the-shelf	May not use space to best advantage	Needs to be securely strapped down
Plastic, flexible	Fresh water, sewage, or fuel	Conforms to odd spaces	Vulnerable to chafe	Cheap and easily installed
Steel, galvanized	Fresh water, sewage	Cheap	Rusts easily if nicked inside	Cement wash or special paint
Steel, stainless	Fresh water, sewage, or fuel	Long lasting, corrosion free	Fairly expensive	No painting needed inside or out

Best Shape for Tanks Tanks for small boats should be deep and narrow whenever possible, to aid in stability when the boat is rolling. The long dimension should lie fore and aft.

Wide, shallow tanks must be well baffled into sections no bigger than 18 inches square to prevent surge.

Cylindrical

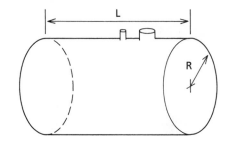

Simple tapering

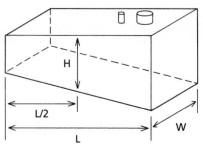

Rectangular

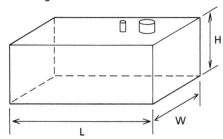

Complex tapering

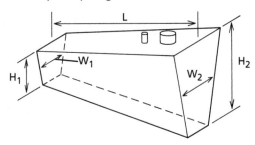

Calculating Tank Capacities Dimensions are in inches. Results are in U.S. gallons.

Cylindrical:
$$L \times 3.14 \times R \times R \div 231 = \text{gallons}$$

Rectangular:
$$L \times H \times W \div 231 = \text{gallons}$$

Simple Tapering:
$$L \times H \text{ (at } L/2\text{)} \times W \div 231 = \text{gallons}$$

Complex Tapering:
$$[(H_1 \times W_1) + (H_2 \times W_2)] \div 2 \times L \div 231 = \text{gallons}$$

Tank Recommendations

➢ Sounding sticks and access hatches should be available for every tank.

➢ Every tank should be thoroughly cleaned at least once a year.

➢ Every tank should have an individual shut-off.

➢ Persistent water in a fuel tank often enters through a mislocated vent outlet.

➢ For reasons of convenience and safety, tanks should be easily removable for maintenance, repair, and cleaning.

VOLUME CONVERSION TABLE

Since almost every country formerly using imperial liquid measures now has gone over to the metric system, all gallons, quarts, and pints listed here are U.S. standard measure unless noted otherwise.

To Convert	to	Multiply by
Gallons imperial	Gallons U.S.	1.20095
Gallons U.S.	Gallons imperial	0.83267
Gallons	Liters	3.785
Gallons	Pints	8
Liters	Gallons	0.2642
Liters	Pints	2.113
Liters	Quarts	1.057
Pints	Gallons	0.125
Pints	Liters	0.4732
Quarts	Liters	0.9463

Examples:

1. 25 gallons to liters:

$$25 \times 3.785 = 94.6 \text{ liters.}$$

2. 250 liters to U.S. gallons:

$$250 \times 0.2642 = 66.05 \text{ gallons}$$

Sails and Helm Balance

For fore-and-aft sails, the trick is to split the sail profiles into triangles. A large mainsail roach would form a tall, skinny triangle—or a set of triangles—all of its own.

The basic formula for the area of a triangle is half the base × perpendicular height.

 When it comes to spinnakers and other balloon headsails, basic triangles provide a fairly close estimate of area, especially if a little informed guesswork is thrown in.

Because no sail is entirely flat, few calculations of sail area are entirely accurate; and for the most part they don't need to be. Complicated sail shapes are better drawn to scale on graph paper for easier estimation of areas.

To calculate the area of a Bermudan mainsail, consider the leech/roach area to be a separate (tall and skinny) triangle.

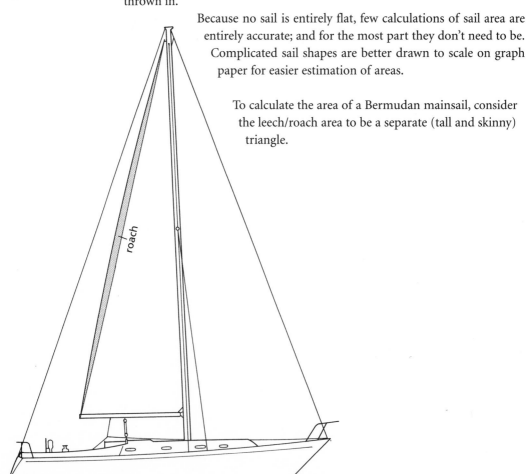

Material	Pros	Cons	Uses
Dacron	Strong, rotproof, relatively cheap	Slight stretch; affected by sunlight	All fore-and-aft sails
Nylon	Stronger than Dacron; rot-proof	Greater stretch than Dacron	Spinnakers and light-weather fore sails
Kevlar	Several times stronger than steel	Expensive; not durable when sharply bent	In laminates for racing and cruising sails
Mylar	Airtight, thin polyester film with no bias	Weaker and more elastic than woven Dacron	In laminates; lighter, stronger than Dacron
Spectra	Even stronger than Kevlar; accepts bending, chafe, fatigue	Tendency to "creep" (elongate) under very heavy sustained load	Racing and cruising sails of all kinds

MAINSAIL SLIDES AND FORESAIL HANKS

➢ Mainsail slides are usually attached about 2 feet (600 mm) apart, with one at or very near the headboard.

➢ Foresail hanks also are fastened about 2 feet (600 mm) apart, with one near the head.

Jamming Slides Mainsail slides will jam in the track if they're seized too firmly to the luff. They must be free to articulate, so that the pull on them comes mostly from above or below as the sail is hoisted or lowered. A shackle, rather than a twine seizing or a length of webbing, automatically provides the freedom of movement needed.

The center of effort (CE) is the geometric center of the sail plan. Its relationship to the boat's center of lateral resistance (CLR) determines, in large part, the balance of the helm. In simplified terms, when the CE is forward of the CLR, the tendency is for the bow to fall off the wind consistently, causing lee helm. When the CE is aft of the CLR, the bow tends to round up into the wind, causing weather helm. Other factors, including the amount of twist in the sails, and their flatness or fullness, also affect helm balance.

Triangular Sails   Find the CE of two triangular sails as follows:

1. Draw lines from the corners of each sail to the middle of the opposite edges. The geometric center of each triangle is at the intersection of those lines.

2. Draw a line between the two geometric centers.

3. From each end of that line, draw perpendiculars projecting in opposite directions. Measure along each perpendicular, to any convenient scale, a number of units proportional to the area of the other sail. Mark those two points.

4. Draw a line between those two points.

The combined center of effort is at the intersection of that line and the original line joining the two geometric centers.

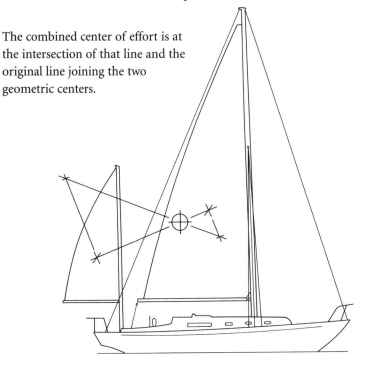

Rectangular Sails To find the CE of a rectangular sail, divide it into two triangles and proceed as above.

For three or more sails, find the combined CE of any two, as above, and use it as one of the two geometric centers in the new calculation.

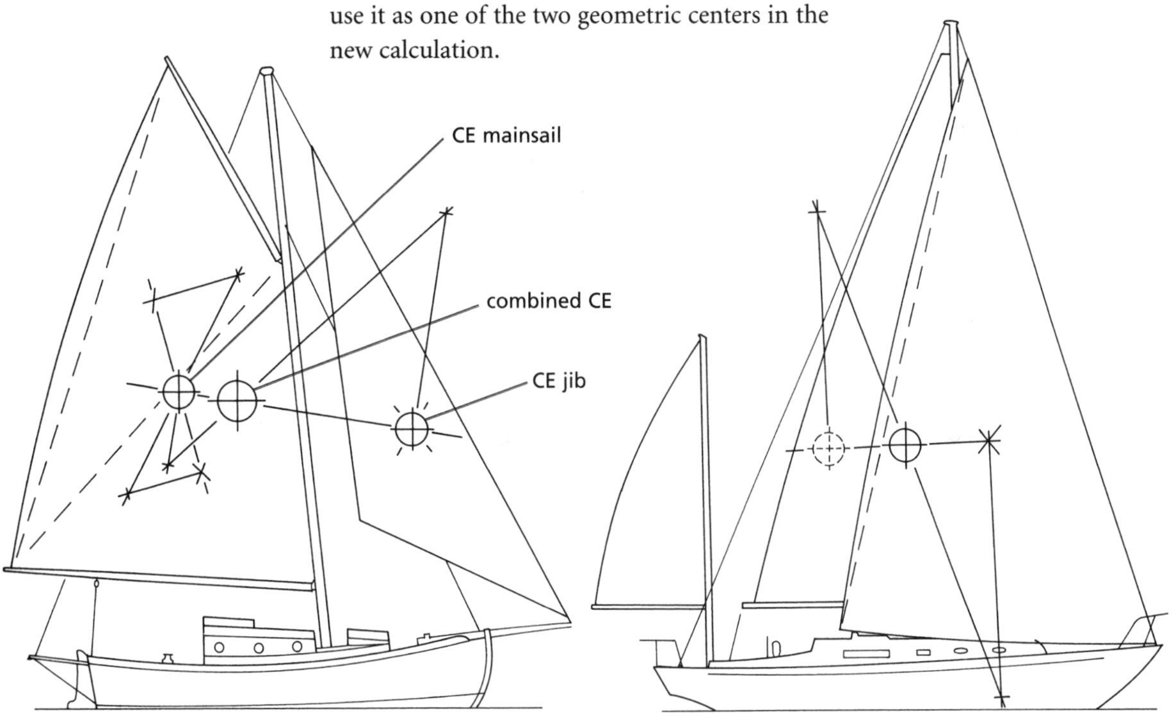

CE mainsail

combined CE

CE jib

PERCENTAGE OF LEAD

In practice, the center of effort (CE) of a vessel's sails should be trailing her center of lateral resistance (CLR), so that she will pivot on her keel and exhibit a slight tendency to turn into the wind at all times.

On the designer's board, though, and for purposes of theoretical discussion, it is customary to show an imaginary CE leading the CLR. (In fact, the effective CLR moves forward to even things out when the boat begins to move.) The amount of this lead, expressed as a percentage of waterline length, varies for different rigs:

Rig	Percentage of Lead
Cutter	13 to 17
Ketch	11 to 14
Schooner	7 to 12
Sloop	13 to 17
Yawl	12 to 15

SAIL AREAS FOR DINGHIES

See graph on page 11.

SAILCLOTH WEIGHT RELATIVE TO BOAT SIZE

 To calculate the weight of sailcloth needed for everyday cruising sails, mainsail and foresail, take one-third of the boat's waterline length in feet and call it ounces per square yard. To convert to ounces per standard U.S. sailcloth measure, or metric measure, see below.

SAILCLOTH CONVERSION CHART

American sailcloth weights are quoted in ounces for an area 36 inches by 28 ½ inches. In other countries, weights are usually quoted either under the old imperial system in ounces per square yard (36 inches by 36 inches) or according to the metric system in grams per square meter. Here's how to convert from one to another:

Imperial	U.S.	Metric	Imperial	U.S.	Metric
18		600	9		300
	14			7	
17		550	8		
	13			6	250
16			7		
				5	
15	12	500	6		200
14			5	4	
	11	450			150
13			4		
	10			3	
12		400	3		100
	9			2	
11			2		
		350		1	50
10	8		1		
			0	0	0

SIZE OF TRYSAIL

A storm trysail should be considerably smaller than a double-reefed mainsail. Its area should be about 5 percent of the square of the length of the unreefed mainsail luff.

Example:

1. Boat's mainsail luff (unreefed) is 36 feet (11 meters) tall.
2. Trysail area in square feet $= 36 \times 36 = 1,296 \times 0.05 = 64.8$ square feet. Round up to 65 square feet.
3. Trysail area in square meters $= 11 \times 11 = 121 \times 0.05 = 6.05$ square meters. Round down to 6 square meters.

SIZE OF STORM HEADSAIL

The recommended area for a spitfire jib or storm staysail on a long-keeled "traditional" cruising yacht is 2.5 percent of the square of the height of the foretriangle.

To maintain proper helm balance in heavy winds, more modern yachts, whose cutaway forefeet encourage the bow to blow to leeward, need either a smaller storm staysail or one carried farther aft on its own stay.

POWER GENERATED BY SAILS

As the wind speed doubles, the force on the sails quadruples. This is the power generated by winds of various strengths:

Wind Strength	Wind Speed in Knots	Pressure in Lb./Sq. Ft.	Horsepower per Sq. Ft.	Pressure in kg per Sq. m	Kilowatts
Force 3	7 to 10	0.28	0.015	1.37	0.118
Force 4	11 to 16	0.67	0.020	3.27	0.161
Force 5	17 to 21	1.31	0.040	6.39	0.312
Force 6	22 to 27	2.30	0.070	11.22	0.559

Thus, in a Force 4 breeze, a 50-square-foot dinghy sail develops a force of 1 horsepower, or a 4.64-square-meter sail develops 0.75 kW.

Spars and Rigging

Minimum specifications for standard keel-stepped aluminum masts with a single pair of spreaders may be derived from the following rule of thumb, based on the length of the spar from deck level to masthead:

Width (transverse section): Length $\div$ 90
Fore-and-aft section: Width $\times$ 1.4
Wall thickness: Width $\div$ 35

length

width   wall thickness

$\longleftarrow$ fore-and-aft section

Example:

1. Mast length from masthead to deck = 56 feet (17 m).
2. Minimum required width = 56 $\div$ 90 = 0.62 feet = 7.44 inches (189 mm).
3. Minimum fore-and-aft section = 7.44 $\times$ 1.4 = 10.42 inches (265 mm).
4. Minimum wall thickness = 7.44 $\div$ 35 = 0.213 inches (5.4 mm).

For heavy-duty offshore cruising, increase the width (transverse section) by 10 to 15 percent, and follow the rule of thumb through as before.

Double-Spreader Rig   For masts with two sets of spreaders, initially calculate all sizes as for the single-spreader rig above. Then reduce only the mast width (transverse section) by 10 to 15 percent. The fore-and-aft section and wall thickness should be the same as for a single-spreader rig.

Deck-Stepped Masts   Use the rule of thumb for keel-stepped masts (above), but divide mast length by 85, instead of 90, to find mast width (transverse section), and then follow through as before.

SPARS & RIGGING

Any mast may vibrate in winds of moderate speeds (5 to 14 miles per hour, or 2 to 6 meters per second), and the vibration may become severe when the natural frequency of the mast coincides with the frequency of vibration.

Alternate sideways movement occurs when wind eddies shed from one side then the other. In theory, it's possible for the mast to vibrate back and forth in any direction perpendicular to the direction of the wind. Almost always, however, the movement is fore-and-aft, with the wind coming from abeam or nearly so.

Here's how to cure, or at least lessen, vibration:

1. First tighten the stays; then tighten the shrouds if necessary.

2. Add a wire or rod inner forestay.

3. For masts with luff-rope grooves (left), hoist a stiff, narrow strip of heavy sailcloth in the mast groove to separate wind eddies. The strip should be at least 4 inches (100 mm) wide.

4. Turn the boat so the wind is striking the bare mast less from the side and more from fore or aft.

5. For temporary relief on small- to medium-size boats, lead a nonstretch line from a strong point forward, such as a Samson post or an anchor cleat, clove-hitch it securely around the mast as high as you can reach, take it to a winch aft, and tighten as much as possible.

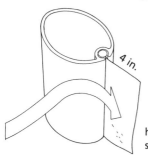

4 in.

heavy
sailcloth

The recommended distance between steps fastened alternately to each side of a mast is 15 to 20 inches (400 to 500 mm). Two steps, one on each side of the mast, should be placed at a height that allows work to be done at the masthead.

SPARS & RIGGING

SPREADER LOCATIONS AND ANGLES

Spreaders should be located at the percentage of mast length given below, measured upward from the deck.

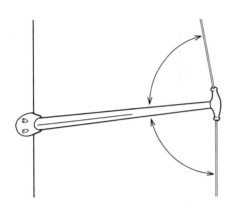

- Single spreader: 50 to 52 percent

- Double spreaders: Lower spreader from 37 to 39 percent

- Upper spreader from 68 to 70 percent

- Angles: All spreaders should exactly bisect the angle formed by the shrouds at their tips.

SHROUD ANGLES

- Angle of any shroud to mast, above the spreader, viewed from fore or aft: never less than 10 degrees.

- Angle between forward lower shroud and mast, viewed from abeam: never less than 5 degrees.

- Angle between aft lower shroud and mast, viewed from abeam: not as critical, but usually 3 to 5 degrees.

MAST AND CHAINPLATE LOADS

- Compression load on mast step, or deck = 1.5 to 2.5 times displacement.

- The load each chainplate should be able to accept separately is about the displacement weight of the boat. The stress on shroud chainplates becomes greater, however, as they move inboard from the gunwale.

- Chainplate loads may be more precisely calculated from the loads on the rigging wires they anchor. Chainplates should comfortably withstand loads 30 to 50 percent greater than those imposed by the wire.

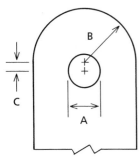

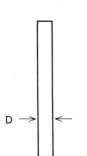

This table is for chainplates of stainless steel or silicon bronze, and produces chainplates or tangs about 33 percent stronger than the compatible stainless steel 1 × 19 rigging wire shown in the table.

Wire Diameter	Breaking Strength	Clevis Pin (A)	Radius (B)	Offset (C)	Thickness (D)
1/8 in.	2,100 lb.	1/4 in.	3/8 in.	1/16 in.	1/8 in.
3 mm	760 kg	6.5 mm	9.5 mm	2 mm	3 mm
5/32 in.	3,300 lb.	5/16 in.	7/16 in.	1/16 in.	3/16 in.
4 mm	1,350 kg	8 mm	11 mm	2 mm	5 mm
3/16 in.	4,700 lb.	3/8 in.	1/2 in.	1/8 in.	3/16 in.
5 mm	2,100 kg	9.5 mm	13 mm	3 mm	5 mm
7/32 in.	6,300 lb.	7/16 in.	9/16 in.	1/8 in.	1/4 in.
1/4 in.	8,200 lb.	1/2 in.	11/16 in.	1/8 in.	1/4 in.
6 mm	3,000 kg	12 mm	17 mm	3 mm	6.5 mm
9/32 in.	10,300 lb.	1/2 in.	11/16 in.	1/8 in.	5/16 in.
7 mm	4,150 kg	14 mm	17 mm	3 mm	8 mm
5/16 in.	12,500 lb.	5/8 in.	13/16 in.	3/16 in.	5/16 in.
8 mm	5,400 kg	16 mm	21 mm	5 mm	8 mm
3/8 in.	17,600 lb.	5/8 in.	7/8 in.	3/16 in.	7/16 in.
9 mm	6,400 kg	18 mm	22 mm	5 mm	10 mm
7/16 in.	23,400 lb.	3/4 in.	1 in.	3/16 in.	1/2 in.
10 mm	8,400 kg	20 mm	25 mm	5 mm	12 mm
1/2 in.	29,700 lb.	7/8 in.	13/16 in.	1/4 in.	1/2 in.
12 mm	12,200 kg	22 mm	30 mm	6 mm	12 mm
9/16 in.	37,000 lb.	7/8 in.	1 1/4 in.	1/4 in.	5/8 in.
14 mm	16,600 kg	23 mm	32 mm	6 mm	16 mm
5/8 in.	46,800 lb.	1 in.	1 3/8 in.	1/4 in.	11/16 in.
16 mm	21,700 kg	25 mm	35 mm	6 mm	17 mm
3/4 in.	59,700 lb.	1 1/4 in.	1 5/8 in.	1/4 in.	3/4 in.
19 mm	27,000 kg	32 mm	41 mm	6 mm	20 mm
7/8 in.	76,700 lb.	1 1/2 in.	1 3/4 in.	5/16 in.	7/8 in.
22 mm	34,500 kg	38 mm	44 mm	8 mm	22 mm

SPARS & RIGGING

BOOM DIAMETER AND THICKNESS

➤ Simple round aluminum boom:
Diameter:	Overall length ÷ 45
Wall thickness:	Diameter ÷ 26

➤ Elliptical-section boom:
Width (transverse section):	Length ÷ 50
Height (vertical section):	Width × 1.5
Wall thickness:	Width ÷ 26

SHROUD ANGLE VS. LOAD

Tension in shrouds accelerates quickly as the angle between shroud and mast diminishes. Mast designers and riggers try to keep the angle at 10 degrees or more, using spreaders to achieve that, if necessary.

In rough terms, a sideways load of 20 pounds (9 kg) at the masthead induces about 240 pounds (108 kg) of tension in a stay with an angle of only 4 degrees. That tension is reduced to about 80 pounds (36 kg) when the stay angle is increased to 12 degrees.

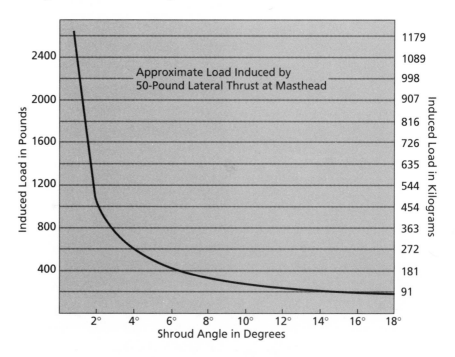

Approximate Load Induced by 50-Pound Lateral Thrust at Masthead

SHROUD STRENGTHS

 Add up the breaking strengths of all shrouds on one side of the boat. The total should equal the boat's displacement multiplied as follows:

Offshore cruisers: Displacement × 1.4

Inshore cruisers: Displacement × 1.2

Racing boats and daysailers: Displacement × 1

Note: In the case of double lower shrouds, use only one lower shroud for this calculation. (The second lower shroud should be the same size as the first, but it is presumed that only one lower at a time carries the load.)

DIVIDING THE SHROUD LOAD

This is how to divide the load between upper and lower shrouds:

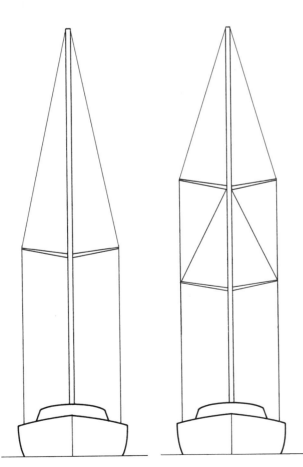

Shroud	Single Spreader	Double Spreader
Lower	60%	48%
Intermediate	—	26%
Upper	40%	26%

Note: When upper and intermediate shrouds join at the lower spreader, and run to a single turnbuckle and chainplate, the combined upper/intermediate shroud should carry 52 percent of the load.

PROPORTIONATE STAY SIZES

Headstay: The size of the heaviest shroud or one size larger.

Backstay: Same size as the headstay.

Note: It's handy for a cruising boat to have all her standing rigging of one size—the size of the heaviest shroud needed.

TURNBUCKLES

Size: For standard, open-body bronze or ordinary stainless steel turnbuckles, the screw diameter should be twice the diameter of the rigging wire.

Opening between jaws The opening between the turnbuckle jaws should be twice the diameter of the rigging wire.

Clevis pin: Twice the diameter of the rigging wire.

Toggles: Always insert toggles between turnbuckle and chainplate, and between mast tang and shroud eye.

toggle

clevis pin

jaw opening

WIRE HALYARD SIZES

All-wire halyards have minimum stretch and are used mainly on racing boats, although there is a growing tendency for them to be replaced by lines made of Spectra, an extremely strong, light fiber from the polypropylene family. Spectra suffers from "creep," which means that a line under strain slowly stretches over a long period of time, so it is better suited to control lines that are adjusted frequently. See "Strength of Rope" later in this chapter.

Here are minimum recommended sizes for 7 × 19 stainless steel wire. Enter this table with the length of the mainsail luff or the headsail leech.

Mainsail Luff or Jib Leech	Main Halyard & Topping Lift	Jib Halyard	Spinnaker Halyard
20 ft.	1/8 in.	5/32 in.	3/16 in.
6 m	3 mm	4 mm	5 mm
25 ft.	1/8 in.	5/32 in.	3/16 in.
7.6 m	3 mm	4 mm	5 mm
30 ft.	5/32 in.	3/16 in.	7/32 in.
9.1 m	4 mm	5 mm	6 mm
35 ft.	5/32 in.	3/16 in.	7/32 in.
10.7 m	4 mm	5 mm	6 mm
40 ft.	3/16 in.	7/32 in.	1/4 in.
12 m	5 mm	6 mm	6 mm
45 ft.	3/16 in.	7/32 in.	1/4 in.
13.7 m	5 mm	6 mm	6 mm
50 ft.	7/32 in.	1/4 in.	9/32 in.
15 m	6 mm	7 mm	7 mm

BREAKING STRENGTH OF 1×19 STAINLESS STEEL WIRE

These figures are for type 302/304 commercial grade wire—the product most commonly used for standing rigging. Type 316 stainless steel wire, recommended for tropical use because of its increased resistance to corrosion, is approximately 15 percent weaker.

Diameter of Wire		Breaking Strength	
Inches	mm	Pounds	kg
1/8	3.2	2,100	953
5/32	3.9	3,300	1,497
3/16	4.8	4,700	2,132
7/32	5.6	6,300	2,858
1/4	6.3	8,200	3,719
9/32	7.1	10,300	4,672
5/16	7.9	12,500	5,670
3/8	9.5	17,600	7,983
7/16	11.1	23,400	10,614
1/2	12.7	29,700	13,472
9/16	14.3	37,000	16,783
5/8	15.9	46,800	21,228

BREAKING STRENGTH OF 7×19 GALVANIZED PLOW STEEL WIRE

Diameter of Wire		Breaking Strength	
Inches	mm	Pounds	kg
3/32	2.4	1,000	454
1/8	3.2	2,000	907
5/32	3.9	2,800	1,270
3/16	4.8	4,200	1,905
7/32	5.6	5,600	2,540
1/4	6.3	7,000	3,175
9/32	7.1	8,000	3,629
5/16	7.9	9,800	4,445
3/8	9.5	14,400	6,532
7/16	11.1	17,600	7,983
1/2	12.7	22,800	10,342

ELASTICITY IN STAINLESS STEEL WIRE

Construction stretch in wire rope is permanent and results from the strands settling into place when the first load is applied. Elastic stretch is temporary, allowing the wire to return to its original length when the load is removed.

 The greater the number of strands in a wire rope, the more elasticity it will have.

Calculating Rigging Load

The elastic stretch of a stainless steel wire increases in rough linear proportion to the load, up to about half the wire's breaking strength. Thus, stretch is a good indication of load.

The following convenient metric formula will give acceptable results with 1 × 19 stainless steel wire:

Load in kilograms = (stretch in centimeters × breaking strength in kilograms) ÷ total length of stretched wire in meters.

Therefore, when a 10-meter (33-foot) wire of any thickness is loaded to half its breaking strength, it will stretch 5 cm (2 inches).

You can use this principle to tune your rigging. Take all the load off a wire and mark on it as accurately as possible with tape or a marking pen a length of 1,980 mm. (If you're not familiar with metric measurements, that's not as much as it sounds—just a little under 6 feet 6 inches.)

Measure the length again as you tighten the turnbuckle. For every millimeter the measured length of 1,980 mm increases, you have loaded the wire with 5 percent of its breaking strength. An increase of 2 mm indicates a healthy 10 percent load. If you ascertain the breaking load of the wire from the table given earlier in this chapter, you can calculate the load in pounds or kilograms, rather than as a percentage.

A load of 25 percent of the breaking strength represents a moderate rig strain, on average. The following graph gives an indication of the elongation at that load per 50 feet (15.24 m) of wire:

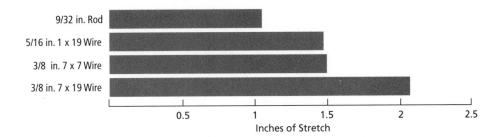

SETTING UP THE RIGGING

The mast should remain perfectly straight under sail, unless it is a fractional-rigged mast purposely designed to bend, or a freestanding mast with no fixed rigging.

After stepping the mast, or rerigging, follow these steps to tension the rig:

1. Give the upper shrouds and the backstay a tension of approximately 10 percent of the boat's displacement. Marine stores stock simple meters (such as the Loos rigging tension gauge) that are accurate enough for this purpose, or you can use the metric stretch formula given above and measure the load yourself.

   You will necessarily induce a tension slightly higher than 10 percent in the forestay because it makes a narrower angle with the mast than does the backstay.

2. Tighten the forward lower shrouds (or babystay) so that the mast bows forward slightly but noticeably at the spreaders.

3. Tighten the aft lower shrouds to straighten the mast again.

4. Sail for a few hours in moderate winds to allow the rig to stretch.

5. Still in a moderate breeze, adjust the mast for straightness according to the diagram on the following page.

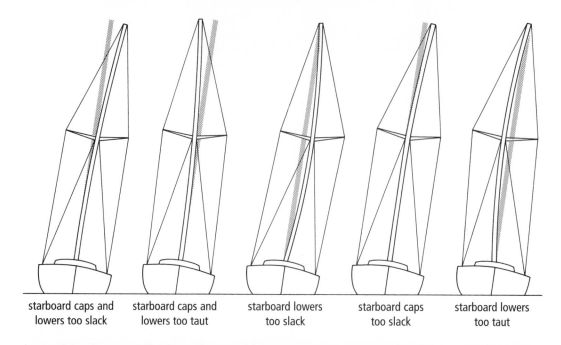

| starboard caps and lowers too slack | starboard caps and lowers too taut | starboard lowers too slack | starboard caps too slack | starboard lowers too taut |

STRENGTH OF ROPE

This table gives conservative breaking strengths of three-stranded rope, except in the case of Spectra, whose strengths are given for double-braid Spectra line covered with Dacron. Single-braid, double-braid, and parallel-core lines may all be considered stronger than ordinary three-stranded line.

Diameter	Manila	Nylon	Dacron	Spectra
3/16 in.	450 lb.	850 lb.	900 lb.	1,600 lb.
5 mm	204 kg	386 kg	408 kg	726 kg
1/4 in.	600 lb.	1,100 lb.	1,200 lb.	3,000 lb.
6 mm	272 kg	499 kg	544 kg	1,361 kg
5/16 in.	1,000 lb.	1,800 lb.	1,800 lb.	4,850 lb.
8 mm	454 kg	816 kg	816 kg	2,200 kg
3/8 in.	1,300 lb.	2,600 lb.	2,600 lb.	6,000 lb.
9 mm	590 kg	1,179 kg	1,179 kg	2,722 kg
7/16 in.	1,700 lb.	3,700 lb.	3,500 lb.	9,700 lb.
11 mm	771 kg	1,678 kg	1,588 kg	4,400 kg
1/2 in.	2,600 lb.	5,000 lb.	4,500 lb.	10,800 lb.
13 mm	1,179 kg	2,268 kg	2,041 kg	4,899 kg
9/16 in.	3,400 lb.	6,400 lb.	5,500 lb.	13,600 lb.
14 mm	1,542 kg	2,903 kg	2,495 kg	6,169 kg
5/8 in.	4,400 lb.	8,000 lb.	6,800 lb.	19,500 lb.
16 mm	1,996 kg	3,629 kg	3,084 kg	8,845 kg
3/4 in.	5,400 lb.	10,500 lb.	9,300 lb.	24,300 lb.
19 mm	2,449 kg	4,763 kg	4,218 kg	11,022 kg
7/8 in.	7,700 lb.	14,000 lb.	12,600 lb.	33,000 lb.
22 mm	3,493 kg	6,350 kg	5,715 kg	14,969 kg
1 in.	9,000 lb.	18,800 lb.	16,100 lb.	43,200 lb.
25 mm	4,082 kg	8,528 kg	7,303 kg	19,596 kg

STRETCH IN FIBER ROPE

Approximate Stretch in Rope at 30 Percent of the Breaking Load

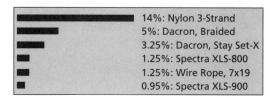

14%: Nylon 3-Strand
5%: Dacron, Braided
3.25%: Dacron, Stay Set-X
1.25%: Spectra XLS-800
1.25%: Wire Rope, 7x19
0.95%: Spectra XLS-900

LINE SIZES FOR RUNNING RIGGING

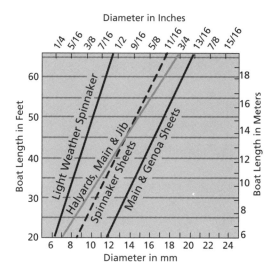

COLOR-CODING OF RUNNING RIGGING

Here is a widely used plan for color-coding halyards, sheets, topping lifts, and other sail control lines:

White: Mainsail
Blue: Jib and genoa
Red: Spinnaker
Green: Topping lifts
Orange: Vangs and travelers

Any tight kink in a fiber line weakens it. For example, any three-strand line that has in the past been stressed to working load or more with a severe kink can be assumed to have lost 30 percent of its strength.

Here's how much the strength of rope may be reduced by various knots. Obviously, the smaller the radius of the knot, the more closely the loss of strength will correspond to the following figures:

Knot	Rope Strength Lost
Anchor bend	24%
Bowline	40%
Clove hitch	40%
Reef knot	55%
Round turn and two half-hitches	30 to 35%
Timber hitch	30 to 35%
Sheet bend	45%

Splices and Wire-Rope Clamps

In fiber rope, a properly tucked and tapered eye splice robs the line of very little strength.

A short splice is the strongest way to join two lines of roughly equal size.

In wire rope, a properly tucked and tapered splice will not reduce the strength of the line.

 Wire-rope clamps, properly applied (with the shaped saddles on the standing part), will reduce a wire's strength by 20 percent.

SPARS & RIGGING

Codes and Signals

 Gun or other explosive signals fired at intervals of about a minute.

 Continuous sounding with any fog signaling apparatus.

 Rockets or shells throwing red stars (not white stars) one at a time at short intervals.

 SOS signals in Morse code by any method, including radio, sound, or light.

"MAYDAY" Spoken word "Mayday" sent by radio.

 The letters N and C in Morse code.

 International code flags N and C in vertical line, with N close on top.

 A rectangular flag or shape with a ball, or anything resembling a ball, below it.

 Open flames, as from a burning bucket of oil or tar.

 Rocket parachute flare showing a red light.

 Handheld flare showing a red light.

Smoke signal giving off orange smoke.

 Raising and lowering outstretched arms slowly and repeatedly.

 Alarm signals from an EPIRB, or radiotelephone.

CODES & SIGNALS

On July 4 and other days nominated by authorities, sailboats dress ship with code flags from water level below the bow to the stern.

Only code flags are used. The ensign, burgee, and other flags are worn in their usual places.

The recommended sequence for a balanced display of color is, from the bow: A, B, 2, U, J, 1, K, E, 3, G, H, 6, I, V, 5, F, L, 4, D, M, 7, P, letter O, 3rd substitute, R, N, 1st substitute, S, T, number 0, C, X, 9, W, Q, 8, Z, Y, 2nd substitute, answering pennant.

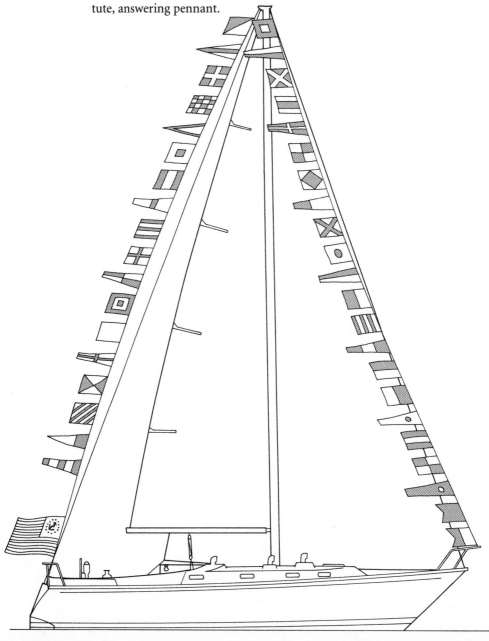

Each letter of The International Code of Signals single-letter code is a complete signal whether transmitted by flags flown singly, by Morse, or by any other method. Their meanings are understood in all languages.

A   I have a diver down; keep well clear at low speed.

B   I am carrying a dangerous cargo.
     [Aboard racing yachts: I am protesting a breach of the rules.]

C   Affirmative. Yes.

D   Keep clear of me; I am maneuvering with difficulty.

E   I am altering course to starboard.

F   I am disabled; communicate with me.

G   I require a pilot.

H   I have a pilot on board.

I   I am altering course to port.

J   I am on fire and have dangerous cargo on board; keep well clear.

K   I wish to communicate with you.

L   You should stop your vessel instantly.

M   I am stopped and making no way through the water.

N   Negative. No.

O   Person overboard.

P   All persons report on board; the vessel is about to proceed to sea.
     [Aboard fishing boats: My nets have come fast upon an obstruction.]

Q   My vessel is healthy, and I request free pratique
     (permission to do business or use a port's facilities).

R   [Spare letter; no meaning assigned.]

S   I am operating stern propulsion.

T   Keep clear of me; I am engaged in pair-trawling.

U   You are running into danger.

V   I require assistance.

W   I require medical assistance.

X   Stop carrying out your intentions and watch for my signals.

Y   I am dragging my anchor.

Z   I require a tow.
     [Aboard fishing boats close together: I am shooting nets.]

CODES & SIGNALS

A	•—	Alpha	N	—•	November	1	•————	Wun		
B	—•••	Bravo	O	———	Oscar	2	••———	Too		
C	—•—•	Charlie	P	•——•	Papa	3	•••——	Tree		
D	—••	Delta	Q	——•—	Quebec	4	••••—	Four		
E	•	Echo	R	•—•	Romeo	5	•••••	Fife		
F	••—•	Foxtrot	S	•••	Sierra	6	—••••	Six		
G	——•	Golf	T	—	Tango	7	——•••	Seven		
H	••••	Hotel	U	••—	Uniform	8	———••	Eight		
I	••	India	V	•••—	Victor	9	————•	Niner		
J	•———	Juliet	W	•——	Whiskey	10	—————	Ten		
K	—•—	Kilo	X	—••—	X-Ray					
L	•—••	Lima	Y	—•——	Yankee					
M	——	Mike	Z	——••	Zulu					

A ship's day was traditionally divided into five full watches of four hours each and two dog watches of two hours each, an arrangement that automatically alternated watches each day.

Starting at noon:

Afternoon watch	Noon to 1600
First dog watch	1600 to 1800
Second dog watch	1800 to 2000
First watch	2000 to midnight
Middle watch	Midnight to 0400
Morning watch	0400 to 0800
Forenoon watch	0800 to noon

From the start of each new watch, one bell was rung for every half hour completed, with a maximum of eight bells. At the end of the first dog watch (1800) four bells were struck as usual, but the second dog watch was treated as a new watch, so at 1830 one bell was struck. At 1900, two bells were struck; at 19:30, three bells; and at 2000, eight bells.

Since 1915, however, U.S. merchant ships over 100 tons gross have divided the crew into three watches working four hours on and eight hours off, combining the two dog watches into one evening watch.

CODES & SIGNAALS

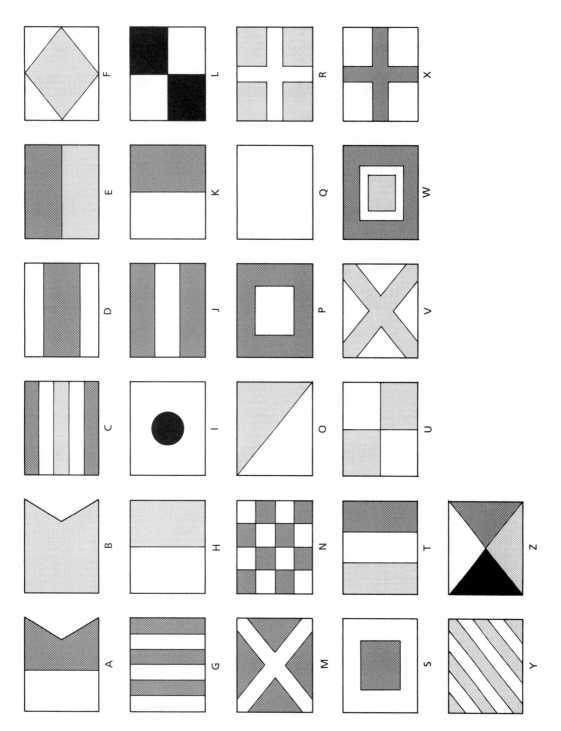

Navigation and Seamanship

BOAT SPEED CALCULATION

 Multiply the length of your boat, in feet, by 0.59, or in meters, by 1.94. The result is your boat's speed factor. Keep it handy. You can use it ever after.

Now throw overboard at the bow something that floats—a piece of orange peel or tissue paper—and note in seconds the time it takes to reach the stern.

Divide the speed factor by that number of seconds.

The result is your boat's speed in knots.

Example:

1. Boat length from bow to stern = 28 feet.
2. Speed factor = 28 × 0.59 = 16.52.
3. Orange peel takes 3.5 seconds from bow to stern.
4. Boat speed = speed factor divided by seconds = 16.52 ÷ 3.5 = 4.72 knots.

Example:

1. Boat length from bow to stern = 9 m.
2. Speed factor = 9 × 1.94 = 17.46.
3. Orange peel takes 5 seconds from bow to stern.
4. Boat speed = 17.46 ÷ 5 = 3.49 knots.

CHART SCALES

Chart Type	Usual Scale	Uses
Harbor	1:10,000 to 1:50,000	Navigating in harbor; magnified detail of channels, wharves, buoys, lights, and anchorages
Coastal	1:50,000 to 1:150,000	Coastal pilotage; good detail of harbor entrances, sea bottom, buoys, lights, and offshore hazards
General	1:150,000 to 1:600,000	Offshore coastal cruising; shows major navigational marks only, but covers large area
Sailing	1:1,200,000 to 1:8,000,000	Long-distance voyaging; route planning for ocean crossings; scant navigational detail
Pilot	1:15,000,000	Ocean route planning; monthly charts show average ocean wind and weather conditions

The 1:40,000 scale is common for small-craft charts and inshore areas.
A nautical mile is about 1.8 inches at this scale.

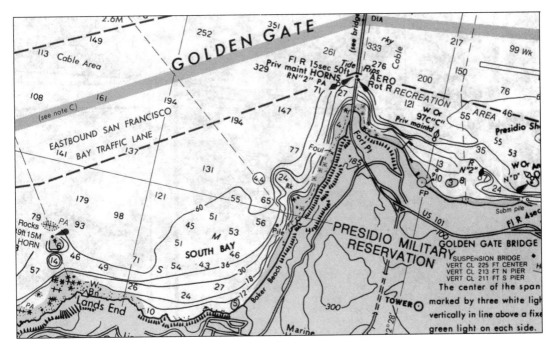

Coastal charts often use the 1:80,000 scale and cover an area roughly 30 by 40 miles.
A nautical mile is about 0.9 inch at this scale.

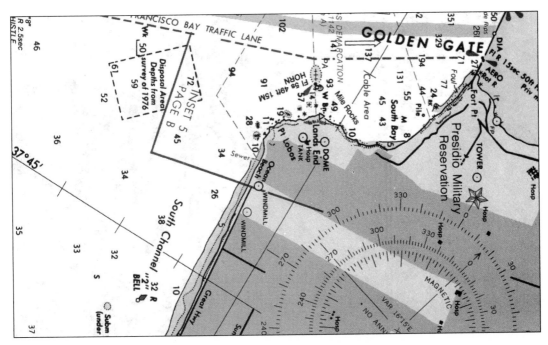

On a clear night, the first or last appearance on the horizon of an identifiable light is a valuable aid to navigation.

If you know your height of eye above sea level, and (from the chart) the height of the light, the following table gives you your distance from the light

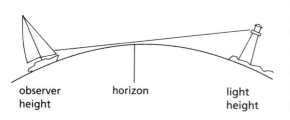

observer height   horizon   light height

with reasonable accuracy. A compass bearing of the light will then provide a position fix.

When the light is actually on the horizon, it will blink on and off as it dips and rises with the boat's movement. If you're in doubt, lower your eye and check that the light dips below the horizon.

Distance in Nautical Miles of Dipping or Rising Light

Height of Light		Height of Eye		
		5 Ft. (1.5 m)	10 Ft. (3 m)	15 Ft. (4.6 m)
40 ft.	12 m	9.75	11	11.75
50 ft.	15 m	10.75	11.75	12.5
60 ft.	18 m	11.5	12.5	13.5
70 ft.	21 m	12.25	13.25	14
80 ft.	24 m	13	14	14.75
90 ft.	27 m	13.5	14.5	15.5
100 ft.	30 m	14	15	16
150 ft.	46 m	16.75	17.75	18.5
200 ft.	61 m	18.75	20	20.75
300 ft.	91 m	22.5	23.5	24.5
400 ft.	122 m	25.5	26.5	27.5

Note: Distances for heights of eye not specified in the table may be interpolated from the figures shown.

Example:

1. Your height of eye above sea level is 8 feet.
2. The light you see dipping below the horizon is on a lighthouse 80 feet above sea level, according to the chart.
3. For 5 feet height of eye, the table shows a distance of 13 nautical miles from the light; for 10 feet height of eye, 14 miles.
4. For 8 feet height of eye, slightly more than halfway between 5 and 10 feet, the distance is slightly more than halfway between 13 and 14 miles—say 13.6 miles.

NAVIGATION & SEAMANSHIP

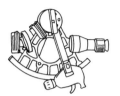

The noon sun sight is the simplest and one of the most useful of all celestial sights. It's valuable even in soundings, particularly when you're running along a north/south coastline.

Noon sights have three advantages over other sights:

➤ No accurate time is needed.

➤ No chart plotting is needed.

➤ The working is very simple.

First determine the greatest altitude of the sun for that day. It's measured with a sextant at local noon simply by taking a succession of sights at short intervals.

Given the sun's greatest altitude, it's a simple matter to work out your latitude. And by running your vessel due east or west along a line of latitude, you can find your way to almost anywhere.

This is the working:

1. Correct the maximum altitude observed on your sextant by allowing for
   (a) **Index error.** This is a usually small, variable sextant error applied to all sights.
   (b) **Dip** (of the sea horizon). Tables in a nautical almanac give dip corrections for the height of your eye above water.
   (c) **Refraction.** This corrects for the "bending" of light rays in the atmosphere. The nautical almanac gives corrections for different angles.
   (d) **Semidiameter.** Depending on whether you shoot the upper or lower limb of the sun, you must add or subtract half its angular diameter—usually 16 minutes are added to a lower-limb shot and subtracted from an upper-limb shot, but more accurate semidiameters are given in the almanac.

   The sum of all these errors is added to, or subtracted from, the observed altitude to determine the true altitude.

2. Subtract true altitude from 90 degrees to find the zenith distance.

3. Add to, or subtract from, the zenith distance the sun's declination, given in the almanac, for the nearest hour of Greenwich mean time. Add when the sun's declination is the same name as your latitude (that is, when both you and the sun are north or south of the equator) and subtract when declination is a different name from latitude.

The result is your latitude in degrees and minutes.

Example:

Your dead-reckoning (DR) latitude: 38° 34′ N

1. 43° 20′   Observed altitude
       − 2′   IE (index error)
       − 3′   Dip (height of eye, 8 feet, 2.4 m)
       − 4′   Refraction
      + 16′   SD (sun's semidiameter)

   43° 27′   True altitude

2. 90° 00′
  − 43° 27′   True altitude

3. 46° 33′   Zenith distance
  − 8° 31′   Sun's declination S. (Subtract when name is different from your latitude. Add when it's the same.)

  38° 02′ N   Your latitude.

FINDING INDEX ERROR (IE)

 Sextant index error can vary frequently, but you can check it easily .

1. Set the sextant to approximately 0° and look toward the sun through the appropriate shades.
2. Two suns will be visible. Adjust the index arm so that the suns' edges just touch; then read the sextant.
3. Reverse the suns, edge to edge again, and read the sextant.
4. One reading will be on the ordinary degree scale; the other will be on the minus side.
5. Subtract the smaller reading from the greater reading, and halve the result. This is the index error.
6. Note the error to the nearest minute. Add it to observed altitude if the error is minus (or off the ordinary scale), and subtract it if the error is positive (or on).

Example:

1. Suns, edge-to-edge, read 34.25′ off the scale.
2. Suns, edge-to-edge reversed, read 30.50′ on the scale.
3. Index error (IE) = 34.25′ − 30.50′ = 3.75′ ÷ 2 = 1.875′ off.
4. Round up to 2′ and add IE of 2′ to every sextant sight.

INDEX ERROR CORRECTION

 If index error exceeds 3', the sextant should be corrected.

PILOT BOOK LIST

U.S. Coast Pilot books provide sailing directions and detailed information for the entire U.S. seacoast. They are intended as companions to specific charts. Here are the separate volumes:

1, Eastport to Cape Cod
2, Cape Cod to Sandy Hook
3, Sandy Hook to Cape Henry
4, Cape Henry to Key West
5, Gulf of Mexico, Puerto Rico, and Virgin Islands
6, [Spare number; no book.]
7, California, Oregon, Washington, and Hawaii
8, Dixon Entrance to Cape Spencer
9, Cape Spencer to Beaufort Sea

The British Admiralty *Sailing Directions*, published in several volumes, are pilot books that cover the world. Many U.S. chart agents stock copies, or will order them for you. Alternatively, you can order direct from one of these sources:

London Yacht Centre
13 Artillery Lane, London E1

Capt. O. M. Watts, Ltd.   J. D. Potter, Ltd.
45 Albermarle Street,   The Minories
London W1   London EC3

Sailing Directions for the Canadian coast, produced by the Canadian Hydrographic Service, are available from:

The Hydrographic Chart Distribution Office
Department of Fisheries and Oceans
P.O. Box 8080, 1675 Russell Road
Ottawa, Ontario
Canada K1G 3H6

They may also be ordered by chart agents or booksellers.

NAVIGATION & SEAMANSHIP

An accurate method of checking compass error is to take a bearing of the sun rising or setting on a sea horizon. Because refraction makes the sun appear to rise before it bisects the horizon, and appear to set afterward, the correct time to take the bearing—whether the sun is rising or setting—is when the sun's lower limb is about half the sun's diameter above the horizon. At that time the center of the sun is actually on the horizon.

No accurate timing is necessary. You need only your latitude to the nearest degree, the sun's declination for the date of your observation—which you'll find in any nautical almanac—and the following amplitude table.

Latitudes 0° to 66°, Declinations 0° to 23°

Your Latitude	Sun's Declination North or South of the Equator											
	1°	3°	5°	7°	9°	11°	13°	15°	17°	19°	21°	23°
0° – 5°	89	87	85	83	81	79	77	75	73	71	69	67
6°	89	87	85	83	81	79	77	75	73	71	69	67
7°	89	87	85	83	81	79	77	75	73	71	69	67
8°	89	87	85	83	81	79	77	75	73	71	69	67
9°	89	87	85	83	81	79	77	75	73	71	69	67
10°	89	87	85	83	81	79	77	75	73	71	69	67
11°	89	87	85	83	81	79	77	75	73	71	69	67
12°	89	87	85	83	81	79	77	75	73	71	69	66
13°	89	87	85	83	81	79	77	75	73	71	68	66
14°	89	87	85	83	81	79	77	75	73	70	68	66
15°	89	87	85	83	81	79	77	74	72	70	68	66
16°	89	87	85	83	81	79	77	74	72	70	68	66
17°	89	87	85	83	81	79	76	74	72	70	68	66
18°	89	87	85	83	81	78	76	74	72	70	68	66
19°	89	87	85	83	81	78	76	74	72	70	68	66
20°	89	87	85	83	80	78	76	74	72	70	68	65
21°	89	87	85	83	80	78	76	74	72	70	67	65
22°	89	87	85	82	80	78	76	74	72	69	67	65
23°	89	87	85	82	80	78	76	74	72	69	67	65
24°	89	87	85	82	80	78	76	74	71	69	67	65
25°	89	87	85	82	80	78	76	73	71	69	67	65
26°	89	87	84	82	80	78	76	73	71	69	67	64
27°	89	87	84	82	80	78	75	73	71	69	66	64
28°	89	87	84	82	80	78	75	73	71	68	66	64
29°	89	87	84	82	80	77	75	73	71	68	66	64
30°	89	87	84	82	80	77	75	73	70	68	66	63

NAVIGATION & SEAMANSHIP

					Sun's Declination North or South of the Equator							
Your Latitude	**1°**	**3°**	**5°**	**7°**	**9°**	**11°**	**13°**	**15°**	**17°**	**19°**	**21°**	**23°**
31°	89	87	84	82	80	77	75	72	70	68	65	63
32°	89	87	84	82	79	77	74	72	70	67	65	63
33°	89	86	84	82	79	77	74	72	70	67	65	62
34°	89	86	84	81	79	77	74	72	69	67	64	62
35°	89	86	84	81	79	76	74	72	69	67	64	62
36°	89	86	84	81	79	76	74	71	69	66	64	61
37°	89	86	84	81	79	76	74	71	69	66	63	61
38°	89	86	84	81	78	76	73	71	68	66	63	60
39°	89	86	84	81	78	76	73	71	68	65	63	60
40°	89	86	84	81	78	75	73	70	68	65	62	59
41°	89	86	83	81	78	75	73	70	67	64	62	59
42°	89	86	83	81	78	75	72	70	67	64	61	58
43°	89	86	83	80	78	75	72	69	66	64	61	58
44°	89	86	83	80	77	75	72	69	66	63	60	57
45°	89	86	83	80	77	74	71	69	66	63	60	56
46°	89	86	83	80	77	74	71	68	65	62	59	56
47°	89	86	83	80	77	74	71	68	65	62	58	55
48°	89	86	83	80	76	73	70	67	64	61	58	54
49°	88	85	82	79	76	73	70	67	64	60	57	53
50°	88	85	82	79	76	73	70	66	63	60	56	53
51°	88	85	82	79	76	72	69	66	62	59	55	52
52°	88	85	82	79	75	72	69	65	62	58	54	51
53°	88	85	82	78	75	72	68	65	61	57	53	50
54°	88	85	82	78	75	71	68	64	60	56	52	48
55°	88	85	81	78	74	71	68	63	59	55	51	47
56°	88	85	81	77	74	70	66	62	59	54	50	46
57°	88	85	81	77	73	70	66	62	58	53	49	44
58°	88	84	81	77	73	69	65	61	57	52	47	43
59°	88	84	80	76	72	68	64	60	55	51	46	41
60°	88	84	80	76	72	67	63	59	54	49	44	39
61°	88	84	80	75	71	67	62	58	53	48	42	36
62°	88	84	79	75	70	66	61	57	52	46	40	34
63°	88	83	79	74	70	65	60	55	50	44	38	31
64°	88	83	78	74	69	64	60	54	48	42	35	27
65°	88	83	78	73	68	63	58	52	46	40	32	22
66°	88	83	78	73	67	63	56	50	44	37	28	16

Note: Calculate the sun's true bearing by advancing away from true north (if the sun is in the northern hemisphere) or true south (if the sun is in the southern hemisphere) by the number of degrees shown in the amplitude tables. At sunrise, advance toward true east. At sunset, advance toward true west.

For even degrees of declination, simple interpolation will suffice.

At the equinoxes, when its declination is 0°, the sun rises due east (090°) and sets due west (270°) in all latitudes.

Example:

1. Your latitude = 48° N. Sun's declination (from the nautical almanac for this particular day) = 19° S.
2. Amplitude (from the preceding table) = 61°.
3. Therefore, sun's amplitude at sunset = S 61° W. The angle is measured from the south because the declination of the sun is south. We measure 61° *west* of south because the sun is ***setting.***
4. The true bearing of the sun is therefore 180° (due south) + 61° = 241°.
5. We'd measure 61° *east* of south if the sun were ***rising,*** and its bearing would be 180° − 61° = 119° true.
6. Compare the sun's true bearing with the bearing you obtained by compass. The difference is variation plus deviation. Variation is shown on the chart. The remaining difference is your compass deviation on your present course.

TACKING DOWNWIND

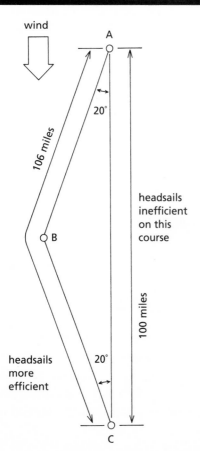

Not only America's Cup racers, but cruisers too, tack downwind. You know why if you've ever rolled your gunwales under for days on end, running dead before the trades.

Sailing 20 degrees off to one side of your rhumb line and then 20 degrees back makes for much more comfortable downwind sailing. And it adds only about 6 percent to the distance covered. But the apparent wind speed increases on the new course, and so should your boat's speed.

If your boat speed goes up from 4 knots to 4.24 knots, for example, you'll arrive at your destination at the same time as the straight-line ETA. If it goes up just one quarter of a knot, from 4 knots to 4.25 knots, you'll get there sooner.

A semidiurnal tide, the type commonly found on the East Coast of America, features two high waters each day of about equal height, and two low waters also about equal. The tide rises (or falls) a predictable amount of its total range in every passing hour. It changes one-twelfth of its range in the first hour, two-twelfths in the second hour, three-twelfths in the third hour, and then tapers off in mirror image for the final three hours. The following chart estimates the comparative height of a tide, above chart datum, at any specific time during the ebb or flow. Note that 50 percent of the water volume increases or decreases in just two hours at midtide.

Hourly changes in tide for a 12-foot range

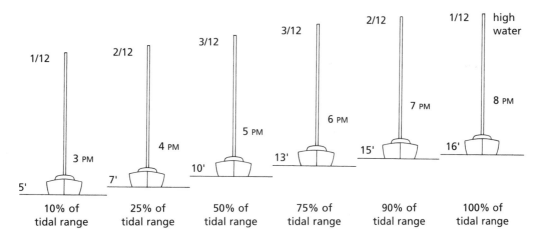

(Low water at 2 P.M. = 4 feet.)

TIME SIGNALS

Time signals for checking the accuracy of a navigator's watch or ship's chronometer may be received on any ordinary shortwave radio.

U.S. stations WWV and WWVH operate continuously on frequencies of 2.5, 5, 10, 15, 20, and 25 MHz.

To convert with confidence from true courses to compass courses and vice versa, remember this mnemonic: Timid Virgins Make Dull Companions; Add Whiskey.

You might want to jot down the initials on every chart you use. They stand for True, Variation, Magnetic, Deviation, and Compass. Add Whiskey means you add westerly values of variation and deviation (and subtract easterly values) when moving from left to right (true to compass). If you know any three of the values, you can work out the other two.

When moving the other way, from right to left (compass to true), *subtract* westerly variation and deviation and add easterly.

Left to right: $+ W, - E$

Right to left: $- W, + E$

T	V	M	D	C
045	20E	025	5W	030

WORLD TIME ZONES

The 24 standard time zones are 15 degrees wide, the arc covered by the sun in one hour. Time zone zero, or Zulu, is centered on the Greenwich meridian in London.

On the opposite side of the world, the international date line approximates the 180th meridian. If you cross the line going west, advance the date by one day. If you're going east, subtract a day.

WEATHER HELM

 Tank testing has shown a small amount of weather helm to be beneficial. With the rudder angled to leeward as much as 4 degrees from the fore-and-aft centerline, useful lift is generated. A rudder turned more than 4 degrees starts acting as a brake, and is detrimental to performance.

NAVIGATION &
SEAMANSHIP

International Time Zones

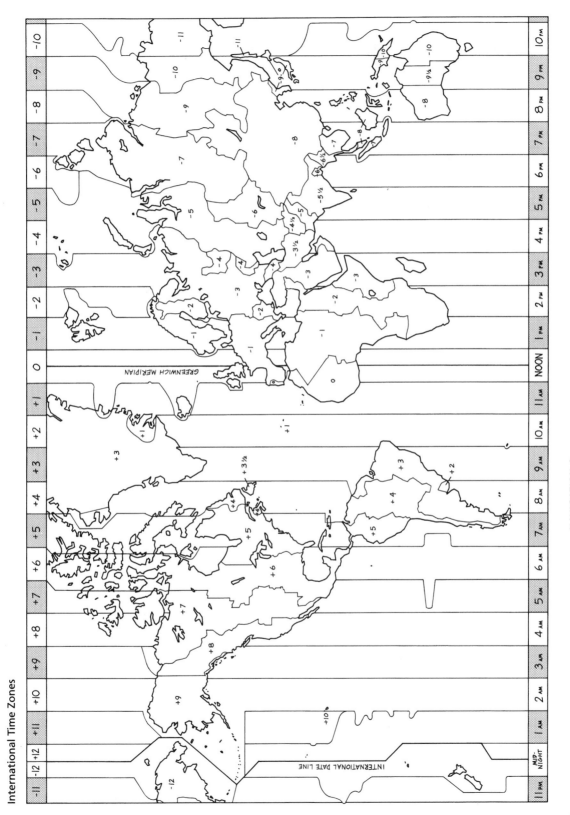

RUDDER STALL ANGLE

Rudder stall usually occurs when the blade is angled about 17 to 20 degrees to the water flow. Any greater angle promotes a full stall and excessive braking.

CAPSIZE SCREENING FORMULA

This is a simplified version of the U.S. Sailing Association's guideline formula for gauging the safety of offshore sailboats:

1. Work out the boat's displacement in cubic feet by dividing her displacement in pounds by 64.
2. Determine the cube root of that number.
3. Now take her beam in feet (and tenths of a foot) and divide it by the cube root you've just obtained.
4. If the answer (the screening number) is less than 2, the boat is considered relatively safe from capsizing in rough water.

Example:

1. Boat displaces 12,500 pounds. Beam is 10 feet 2 inches. Displacement in cubic feet = 12,500 ÷ 64 = 195.31.
2. Cube root of 195.31 = 5.802.
3. Beam = 10.17 feet. 10.17 ÷ 5.802 = 1.75.
4. Since the screening number is less than 2, this boat passes the capsize screening test.

SEA ANCHORS

Some of the world's most experienced long-distance cruisers recommend the use of a sea anchor and a trysail to heave to in violent gales and storms. While powerboats and even shallow-draft centerboard sailing boats will often lie quietly to a sea anchor streamed from the bow, few deep-keeled cruising sailboats will lie bow to the seas in this fashion.

But by deploying a parachute sea anchor on a bridle, the bow of a sailboat may be angled to within 50 degrees of the wind and waves, and the boat's forward motion checked. She will then lie directly to leeward of the turbulent currents caused by her sideways drift through the water. This "slick" apparently encourages approaching waves to trip, plunge, and dissipate most of their energy before hitting the boat. Because every hull reacts differently and because sea conditions vary widely, the best combination of sails, and the best sea-anchor size and position, must be found by experiment.

Boat Length	Parachute Diameter	Line Size	Chain Size_
Up to 20 ft.	6 ft.	1/4 in.	1/4 in.
6 m	1.8 m	6.5 mm	6.5 mm
20–25 ft.	9 ft.	3/8 in.	1/4 in.
6–7.6 m	2.7 m	9 mm	6.5 mm
25–35 ft.	12 ft.	1/2 in.	5/16 in.
7.6 –10.6 m	3.6 m	13 mm	8 mm
35–40 ft.	15 ft.	5/8 in.	3/8 in.
3.6–12 m	4.5 m	16 mm	9 mm
40–50 ft.	18 ft.	5/8 in.	3/8 in.
12–15 m	5.5 m	16 mm	9 mm
50–100 ft.	24 ft.	3/4 in.	1/2 in.
15–30 m	7.3 m	20 mm	13 mm

STABILITY FROM ROLL TIME

The time it takes a sailboat to roll from gunwale to gunwale and back in still water under bare masts is an indication of her stiffness.

Roll time can be ascertained fairly accurately on a calm day at the dock. Get some helpers to press down hard on the gunwale in unison until the boat is rolling as hard as she can. Have a stopwatch ready. Stop pushing when the boat is at the bottom of her roll toward the dock, and time her roll from this position back to this position, or as far back as she will come.

Time her roll to the nearest tenth of a second. If you time 10 rolls, one after another, and average the result, the roll time will be more accurate.

Then multiply the roll time in seconds by the boat's widest beam (not necessarily the waterline beam) measured in meters. Check the result against the following list. If it is substantially different from what you find here, seek professional advice before operating the boat offshore.

Roll Time × Beam	Boat Type
0.95	Heavy-displacement cruisers, 25 percent or less ballast ratio, no high deckhouse or cabintop
0.90	Heavy cruisers, 25 to 35 percent ballast ratio, nothing unusual on deck
0.85	Medium-displacement cruisers, 35 percent or more ballast ratio, no high cabins
0.80	Cruiser/racers, 35 percent or more ballast ratio, moderate draft and moderate cabintop height
0.75	Racers, 40 percent or more ballast ratio, deep draft, low cabintops
0.70	Fringe racers, 45 percent or more ballast ratio, extra-deep keels

PHRF Race Handicapping System

The Performance Handicap Racing Fleet seeks to promote fair racing between different kinds of sailboats by allocating a rating based on past performance.

The rating assigned to a boat is a comparative allowance expressed in seconds per mile. For example, a yacht with a PHRF rating of 184 will give 11 seconds per mile to a competitor rated at 195. In other words, the handicappers regard the yacht as inherently faster by 11 seconds a mile.

Watch System for Yachts

This is a popular 24-hour crew schedule for oceangoing yachts, based on the Swedish watch system, which begins and ends at 1900, splitting the day into watches of five, four, four, five, and six hours. The advantage of this modified version is that it provides occasional long periods of rest. Its disadvantage is that it demands extralong deck duty while the watch below is resting. Although this system works well in trade-wind climates and calm seas, shorter watches (usually four hours maximum) are advisable in higher latitudes, especially when a vessel is shorthanded.

Time	Port Watch	Starboard Watch
0000	On	Off
0100	On	Off
0200	On	Off
0300	On	Off
0400	Off	On
0500	Off	On
0600	Off	On
0700	Fix breakfast	On
0800	On	Off
0900	On	Off
1000	On	Off
1100	On	Off
1200	On	Fix lunch
1300	Off	On
1400	Off	On
1500	Off	On
1600	Off	On
1700	On	Fix supper
1800	On	Off
1900	On	Off
2000	On	Off
2100	On	Off
2200	On	Off
2300	On	Off

Port and starboard watches are automatically reversed every 24 hours.

NAVIGATION & SEAMANSHIP

Weather

Scale #	Wind Speed	Description	Effect at Sea	Effect on Land
0	0 knots 0 mph 0 km/h	Calm	Sea like a mirror. Sailboat becalmed.	Smoke rises vertically.
1	1–3 knots 1–3 mph 1–5 km/h	Light air	Slight ripples. Yacht just has steerage way.	Smoke drift indicates wind direction.
2	4–6 knots 4–7 mph 6–11 km/h	Light breeze	Small wavelets. Wind just keeps sails full.	Leaves rustle. Wind felt on face.
3	7–10 knots 8–12 mph 12–19 km/h	Gentle breeze	Larger wavelets, few whitecaps. Yachts begin to heel.	Light flags extended. Leaves in constant motion.
4	11–16 knots 13–18 mph 20–28 km/h	Moderate breeze	Small waves, many whitecaps. Yachts sail with decided list, and start to dip gunwales.	Small branches move. Leaves, dust, shreds of paper lifted off the ground.

Scale #	Wind Speed	Description	Effect at Sea	Effect on Land
5	17–21 knots 19–24 mph 29–38 km/h	Fresh breeze	Moderate waves, longer in form. Spray starts to fly. Small yachts take in first reef.	Trees start to sway. Crested wavelets form on inland waters.
6	22–27 knots 25–31 mph 39–49 km/h	Strong breeze	Larger waves, 8 to 12 ft. Yachts double-reef mainsails. Heavier spray.	Large branches sway. Umbrellas used with great difficulty.
7	28–33 knots 32–38 mph 50–61 km/h	Near gale	Foam from breaking waves starts blowing in streaks. Yachts hoist trysails and storm jibs.	Whole trees in motion. Difficult to walk against the wind.
8	34–40 knots 39–46 mph 62–74 km/h	Gale	Waves 12 to 20 ft. high, edges of crests break into spindrift. Yachts adopt storm tactics.	Twigs break off trees. Progress on foot generally impeded.
9	41–47 knots 47–54 mph 75–88 km/h	Strong gale	Reduced visibility because of flying spray. High waves; sea begins to roll.	Damage to structures. Roofing materials torn loose from houses.
10	48–55 knots 55–63 mph 89–102 km/h	Storm	Waves to 30 ft. with over-hanging crests. Sea appears white. Waves break forcefully.	Seldom experienced inland. Trees uprooted and homes destroyed.

WEATHER

Scale #	Wind Speed	Description	Effect at Sea	Effect on Land
11	56–63 knots 64–72 mph 103–117 km/h	Violent storm	Waves to 45 ft. White foam patches cover sea. Edges of waves turn frothy.	Very rarely experienced inland. Widespread damage.
12	64 + knots 73 + mph 118 + km/h	Hurricane	Waves over 45 ft. Air filled with foam. Sea appears completely white.	Hurricanes lose energy inland and downgrade to storms.

GLOBAL AIR CIRCULATION

Heated air rises along the equator and flows outward toward the poles, descending along the way and being deflected by the spinning of the Earth. This diagram shows the theoretical circulation.

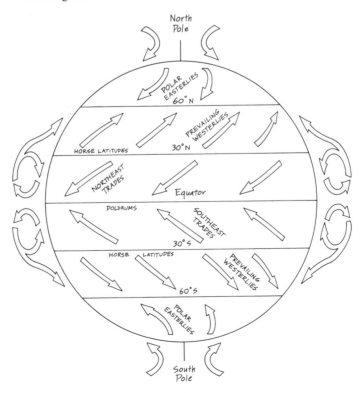

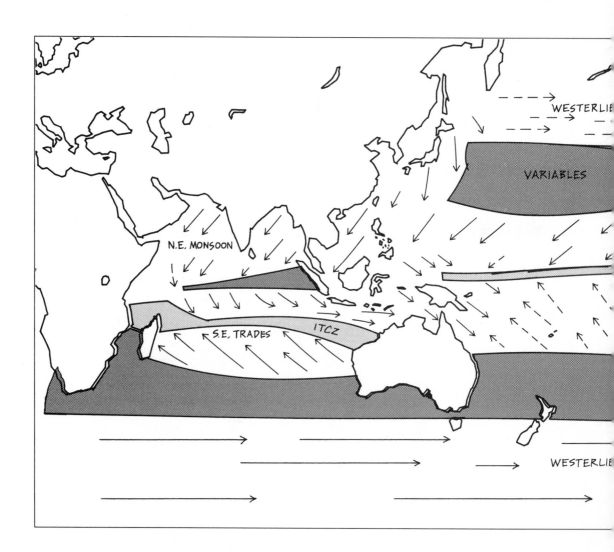

WEATHER

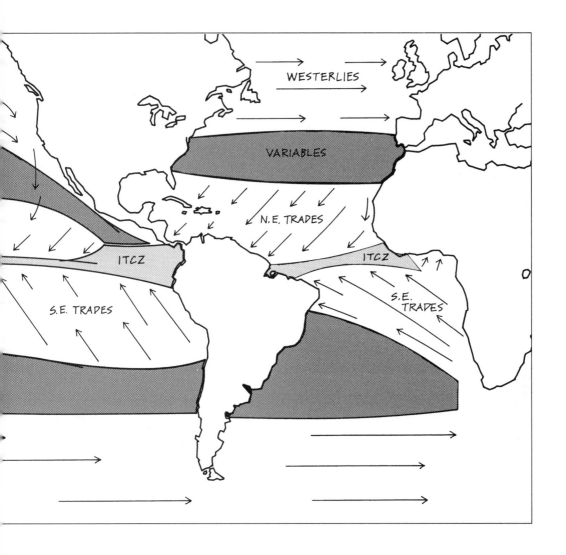

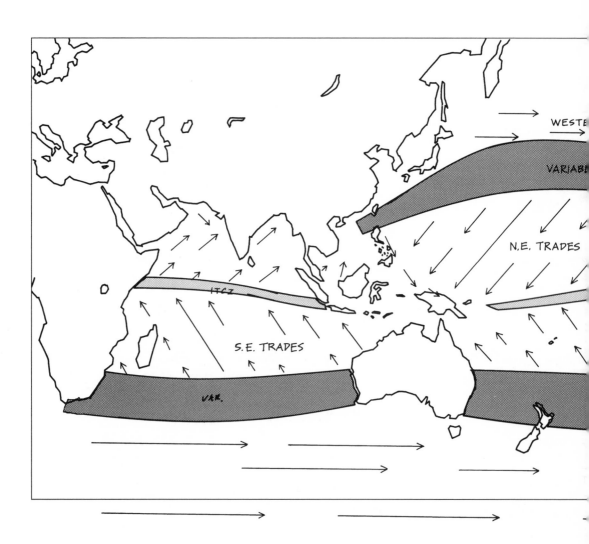

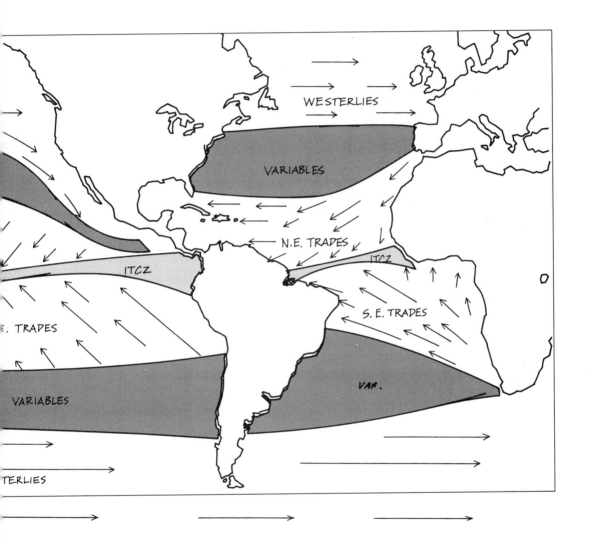

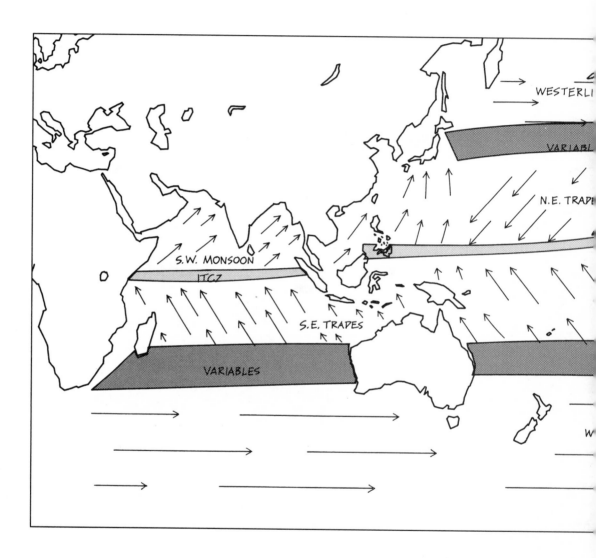

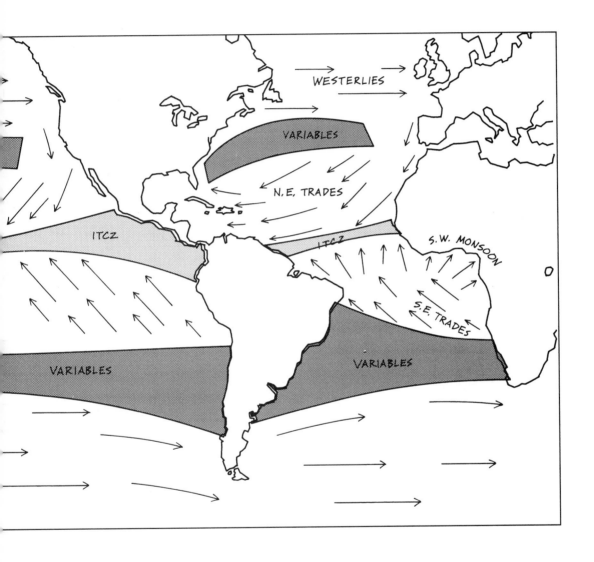

WESTERLIES

VARIABLES

N.E. TRADES

ITCZ

ITCZ

S.W. MONSOON

S.E. TRADES

VARIABLES

VARIABLES

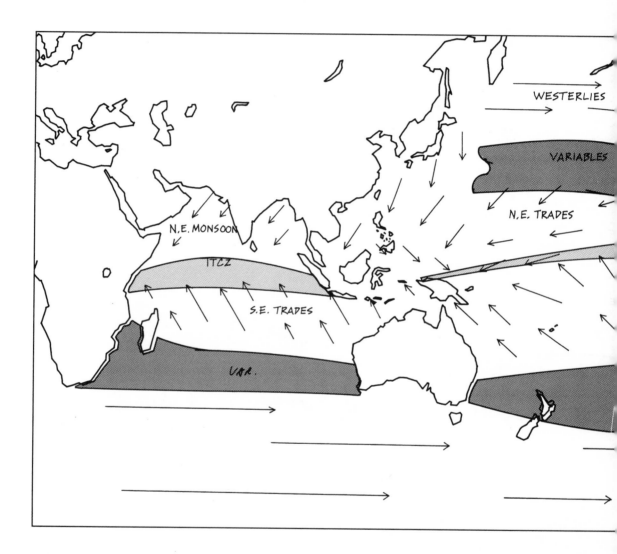

WESTERLIES

VARIABLES

N.E. TRADES

N.E. MONSOON

ITCZ

S.E. TRADES

VAR.

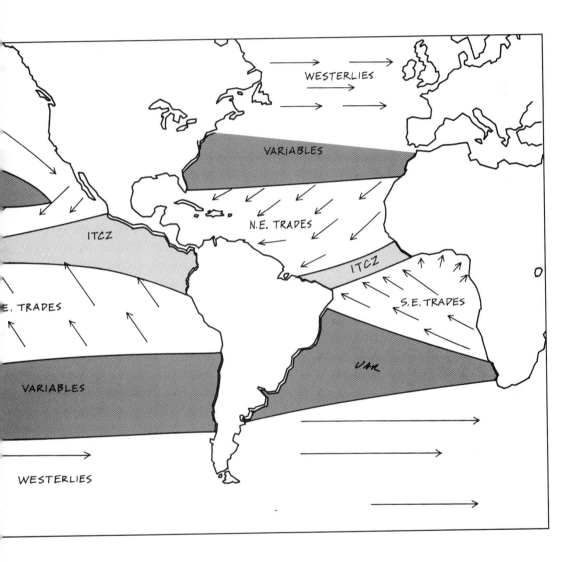

WORLD DISTRIBUTION OF TROPICAL STORMS

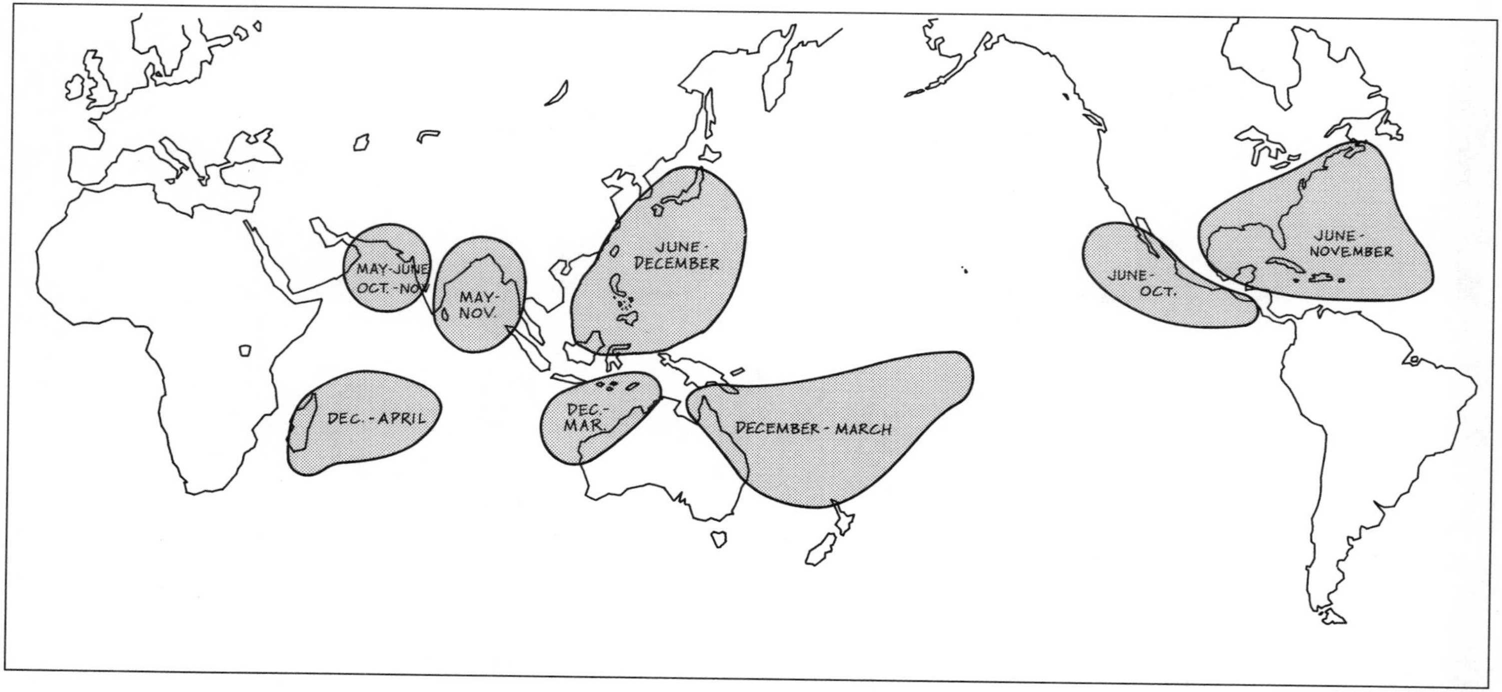

JUNE-NOVEMBER

JUNE-OCT.

DECEMBER-MARCH

JUNE-DECEMBER

DEC.-MAR.

MAY-NOV.

MAY-JUNE OCT.-NOV.

DEC.-APRIL

When you face the wind in the northern hemisphere, the center of an approaching low-pressure area (depression) lies between 90 degrees and 135 degrees on your right. Atmospheric pressure increases on your left.

South of the equator, the low pressure is 90 to 135 degrees on your left when you face the wind, and barometric pressure increases on your right.

HURRICANE STRATEGY

northern hemisphere

dangerous semicircle

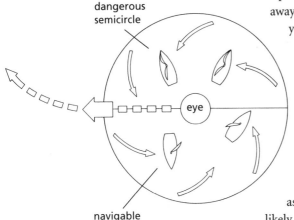

navigable semicircle

navigable semicircle

dangerous semicircle

southern hemisphere

If you are caught in the direct path of an approaching tropical storm in the northern hemisphere, the conventional strategy is to run off on the starboard tack, keeping the wind on the starboard quarter. This will take you away from the dangerous center of the depression and move you into the "safe" semicircle of the storm.

A rapidly falling barometer, combined with a wind direction that remains steady, indicates that you are in the direct path.

If the approaching storm will pass to your right as you face its center, you are in danger of being caught in the dangerous semicircle. The wind will veer—that is, shift clockwise—as the storm approaches. In that case, you should sail close-hauled on the starboard tack at right angles to the assumed track of the storm. Alternatively—and more likely if you are close to the center—you should heave to on the starboard tack.

If, when facing the approaching storm, you judge its center will pass to your left, you are in the "safe" or "navigable" semicircle. Your judgment will be confirmed if the wind begins to back, that is, shift counterclockwise. In that case, you should run with the wind on the starboard quarter, keeping a course at right angles to the storm track and away from its center, as far as possible.

In the southern hemisphere, tropical storms rotate the opposite way—their dangerous semicircles are on the left of the storm track.

WEATHER

Weather bombs are extratropical cyclones that deepen extremely quickly, covering a broad area and building up high winds and very dangerous seas. They have the same effect as hurricanes.

A bomb is defined as a low in which pressure falls at least one millibar per hour for 24 hours.

They can occur almost anywhere in the world, but most develop in the Atlantic, in the Gulf Stream or just north of it, and in the Kuroshio Current in the Pacific.

The infamous 1979 Fastnet storm in Britain was one such weather bomb. The 1994 "Queen's Birthday" storm that swept the Pacific north of New Zealand was another.

BAROMETER CONVERSIONS

Millibars	Inches		Millibars	Inches
960	28.35		1005	29.68
965	28.50		1010	29.83
970	28.65		1015	29.97
975	28.79		1020	30.12
980	28.94		1025	30.27
985	29.09		1030	30.41
990	29.23		1035	30.57
995	29.38		1040	30.71
1000	29.53		1045	30.86

In middle latitudes, a high barometer reads about 1033 mb, or 30.50 inches. A low barometer reads about 999 mb, or 29.50 inches. The average reading at sea level is about 1013 mb, or 29.90 inches.

Multiply inches of mercury by 33.86 to convert to millibars.

Multiply millibars by 0.0295327 to convert to inches of mercury.

WEATHER

Flags by day, and lights by night, are displayed at Coast Guard stations, some municipal marinas, and most yacht clubs to indicate heavy weather conditions. Do not rely solely on such flags for warnings, however, because this system, particularly that part of it run by government agencies, is subject to fluctuations in funding.

Weather warning signals

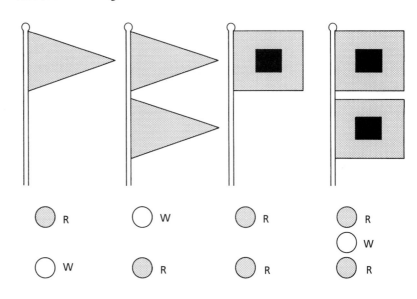

WEATHER WARNING TERMS

Small-Craft Advisory Winds up to 33 knots (38 mph, 61 km/h) and/or sea conditions dangerous to small craft are forecast for the area.

Gale Warning Winds ranging from 34 to 47 knots (39 to 54 mph, 62 to 87 km/h) are forecast.

Storm Warning Winds of 48 knots (55 mph, 88 km/h) and above are forecast.

Hurricane Warning Winds of 64 knots (74 mph, 119 km/h) and above are forecast.

The National Weather Service defines "small craft" as "small boats, yachts, tugs, barges with little freeboard, or any other low-powered craft."

Small-craft advisories forecast the worst weather conditions expected in the forecast period, no matter how long they may last nor how localized they may be in any portion of the whole forecast area. They should be supplemented with local observations and advice whenever possible.

WEATHER

Wind Direction	Barometer Reading	Barometer Movement	Weather Outlook
SW to NW	1023 / 30.2	Steady	Continuing fair. Temperature remaining steady.
SW to NW	1023 / 30.2	Slow fall	Temperature rising slowly. Fair for 48 hours.
SW to NW	1019 to 1023 30.1 to 30.2	Steady	Stable temperature, remaining fair for 24 to 48 hours.
SW to NW	1019 to 1023 30.1 to 30.2	Rapid rise	Continuing fair but becoming increasingly cloudy. Rain and cooler within 48 hours.
SE to S	1019 to 1023 30.1 to 30.2	Slow fall	Rain and warmer within 24 hours.
SE to S	1019 to 1023 30.1 to 30.2	Rapid fall	Wind and rain increasing within 12 to 18 hours.
E to S	1009 or less 29.8 or less	Rapid fall	Severe storm imminent, clearing within 24 hours. Winter: dropping temperatures.
NE to E	1019 and higher 30.1 and higher	Slow fall	Summer: light winds, rain within 3 days. Winter: rain within 24 hours. Slightly warmer.
NE to E	1019 and higher 30.1 and higher	Rapid fall	Summer: rain within 24 hours. Winter: increasing rain or snow within 12 hours.
NE to SE	1019 to 1023 30.1 to 30.2	Slow fall	Wind and rain increasing within 12 to 18 hours.
NE to SE	1019 to 1023 30.1 to 30.2	Rapid fall	Wind and rain increasing within 12 hours.
NE to SE	1016 and less 30.0 and less	Slow fall	Extended period of rain, 1 to 3 days or more.
NE to SE	1016 and less 30.0 and less	Rapid fall	Strong winds and rain imminent. Clearing and cooling within 36 hours.
N to E	1009 and less 29.8 and less	Rapid fall	Northeast gale and heavy rain imminent. Winter: Snow and extended colder weather.
E to S	1009 and less 29.8 and less	Rapid fall	Severe storm imminent. Winter: clearing and colder within 24 hours.
S to SW	1016 or less 30.0 or less	Slow rise	Clearing within a few hours. Fair weather for several days.

Note: A rapid rise or fall is one in which barometric pressure changes at a rate of 1 millibar (0.03 inches) every 3 hours or less.

WEATHER

Knowing which type of fog you're experiencing can help you guess when it will clear. Here are the four most common types of fog experienced by sailors:

Radiation Fog   Radiation fog forms in near-calms on clear nights, when the ground radiates its heat into space and cools down. Moisture in warmer air passing over the cool land may condense as fog and drift out over water. Should dissipate in early morning.

Advection Fog   Advection fog forms when warm, moist air from any source flows over colder water. Given the right conditions—such as warm air from a stationary Bermuda High flowing over the cold waters of the Labrador Current, the Grand Banks, and the Gulf of Maine—this fog can persist for days.

Steam Fog   Steam fog, or sea smoke, forms when cold air flows across warmer water. Usually short-lived.

Precipitation Fog   Precipitation fog forms when warm rain falls through a lower layer of cold air. Usually short-lived.

This table gives wind pressure in pounds:

Frontal Area (Sq. Ft.)	Wind Speed			
	30 Knots	60 Knots	80 Knots	100 Knots
1	3	13	22	32
50	150	630	1,115	1,600
150	450	1,890	3,345	4,860
200	600	2,520	4,460	6,480

Note: Multiply square feet by 0.0929 to convert to square meters. Multiply pounds by 0.4536 to convert to kilograms.

WEATHER

Safety

➤ Horseshoe lifebuoys, at least two, ready for throwing.

➤ A crew-overboard pole, weighted to float upright, with a flag on top and a self-igniting light attached. It should preferably be made fast to one of the lifebuoys.

➤ Floating line, at least 100 feet (30 m) long, within easy reach of the person at the helm. It should withstand a load of at least 1,000 pounds (450 kg).

➤ Means to get a person back on board—a ladder with at least two rungs under water; a rubber dinghy; or a sling and a handy-billy hoist.

➤ A loran or GPS, to mark your position and guide you back to the spot.

➤ A radio, to call for outside help.

➤ A Lifesling, with optional hoisting tackle. This special lifebuoy, deployed at the end of a long line, is towed in a circle around the crew in the water until contact is made. It has a built-in harness to which the hoisting tackle may be secured.

CREW-OVERBOARD PROCEDURE

1. Shout "Crew overboard!" to alert the crew.

2. Throw overboard horseshoe lifebuoys and anything else in the cockpit likely to provide flotation or mark the spot. Heave a Lifesling buoy overboard.

3. Detail someone to point at the person in the water and keep pointing, no matter what.

4. Press the button on your GPS or loran that saves your position.

5. Note your compass course; then turn the boat back on a reciprocal course as quickly as possible. It is very important not to get too far away from the victim.

6. Approach cautiously and be prepared to cut power to avoid propeller injuries.

SAFETY

7. In one end of a line capable of supporting the victim's weight, tie a bowline to slip over the victim's head and shoulders. (This will probably not be needed if you are using a Lifesling and the victim is correctly attached to the buoy.)

8. Haul the victim out of the water any way you can—into a dinghy, onto the deck, or into the cockpit, with a halyard, ladder, block and tackle, or with sheer crew muscle. On a racing boat on a calm day, it may be possible to lower the mainsail into the water and roll the victim aboard in the bunt.

9. Treat the victim as necessary for water inhalation, shock, hypothermia, or heart failure.

10. Radio for medical advice or broadcast a Mayday call if warranted.

Note: Every member of the crew should learn, and regularly practice, a crew-overboard routine.

FIRE EXTINGUISHERS

Portable extinguishers must be marked with a U.S. Coast Guard approval number and must be mounted in the special bracket normally sold with the extinguisher.

Extinguishers are classified by letter symbols as fit for use against Type A, B, or C fires (see below). Their relative size is indicated by the designation B-I or B-II.

Class	Carbon Dioxide (CO_2)	Chemical
B-I	4 lb.	2 lb.
B-II	15 lb.	10 lb.

Note: Halon gas, one of the best fire extinguishers for small boats, has not been manufactured for this specific use since January 1994 because it is suspected of depleting the ozone layer.

Nevertheless, new halon extinguishers are available at marine stores, and may continue to be for some years, while halon already in existence is recycled from large firefighting systems.

Halon is very expensive, but it is particularly effective in extinguishing engine-room fuel fires. Instructions for the use and maintenance of halon extinguishers are similar to those listed below for carbon dioxide (CO_2).

SAFETY

145

Types of Fire
Type A fires: Ordinary combustibles: cardboard, cloth, paper, many plastics, rubber, and wood.

Type B fires: Flammable liquids: cooking fat, gasoline, grease, oil (vegetable and mineral), some paints, and solvents.

Type C fires: Electrical equipment: appliances, fuse boxes, outlets, wiring—anything that might carry a lethal electrical current.

Extinguishing Methods
Three basic ways to extinguish a fire are:

➤ Cool the burning material.

➤ Smother the fire and starve it of oxygen.

➤ Remove the combustible material.

Extinguisher Varieties and Uses

	Carbon Dioxide Extinguisher	Dry Chemical Extinguisher
Effective on fire types:	A, B, and C.	A, B, and C.
How it works:	Smothers fire. Also has slight cooling effect.	Smothers fire. Also has chemical reaction that inhibits flames.
Maintenance (check label):	Weigh every six months. Service after weight drops by 10 percent. Loosen powder frequently with vigorous shaking and/or by striking base.	Check visual pressure indicator. Or weigh every six months.
Residue:	None.	Fine powder. May corrode metals if not promptly cleaned after fire.
Warnings:	• Keep bare hand away from freezing discharging gas. • May irritate lungs if breathed too long. • First discharge at close range tends to cause spreading of Type B fires.	• Fine powder may reduce visibility. • Beware of oxygen depletion in small rooms or closed areas. • Efficiency affected by wind or dispersing drafts.

SAFETY

Notes:

- ➤ Water, salt or fresh, is very effective on most Type A fires. Keep a galvanized steel bucket on board.

- ➤ Type B fires (oil, gasoline, kerosene, diesel fuel, and cooking fat) must be put out with a carbon-dioxide or dry-chemical extinguisher.

- ➤ Extinguishers should be kept near places where fire is most likely to break out—but not right at those spots. It would be dangerous, for example, to reach across a burning oil fire in the galley to grab the extinguisher.

- ➤ Most extinguishers found on small boats have a discharge time of between 8 and 20 seconds. Use each second wisely.

Firefighting Golden Rules

These are the three golden rules for fighting fires:

1. Don't delay.
2. Get close.
3. Aim at the base of the fire and sweep continuously from side to side.

Portable Fire Extinguishers in Relation to Boat Size

Boat Size	Extinguishers Required
Less than 26 ft.	One B-I
26 to 40 ft.	Two B-Is or one B-II
40 to 65 ft.	Three B-Is, or one B-II and one B-I

Note: These are the Coast Guard's minimum requirements for boats with inboard engines and permanently installed fuel tanks, or closed compartments in which portable fuel tanks are stored. Prudent skippers will carry at least one more B-I or B-II extinguisher.

Improvised Fire Extinguishers

All these home remedies work by smothering a fire:

- ➤ Baking soda
- ➤ Salt
- ➤ Flour
- ➤ Sand
- ➤ Wet blanket
- ➤ A tight-fitting lid slid over a flaming saucepan or frying pan

Type	Height	Burn Time	Candlepower	Night Range
12-gauge meteor	200–325 ft. 60–100 m	6 seconds	10,000	10 miles 16 km
25-mm (1 in.) meteor	375–500 ft. 115–150 m	6–10 seconds	10,000	10–12 miles 16–20 km
25-mm (1 in.) red parachute	1,000 ft. 300 m	25–40 seconds	10,000 – 30,000	20–25 miles 30–40 km

Note: Some meteor flares are fired from a pistol; others are self-launching, like parachute flares. Meteors rise to 375 to 500 feet and burn for 6 to 10 seconds. Parachute flares use a rocket to gain altitude. They go higher, burn brighter, and last longer.

EMERGENCY HAND TOOLS FOR OFFSHORE CRUISERS

Ax, small
Bolt cutters, large
Brace, with bits to 1 inch
C-clamps, several
Drill, hand, 3/8-inch, and bits
Duct tape
Electrician's tape
Files, triangular, flat, and round
Hammer, ballpeen
Metal snips
Plane, small
Pliers, needlenose, ordinary, and Vise-Grips
Rasp, shoemaker's (flat and half-round; coarse and medium)
Saws, ordinary crosscut, and hacksaw with standard and carbide blades
Screwdrivers, ordinary slot, and Phillips-head
Stainless steel seizing wire
Wire clamps
Wood chisels, 1/2-inch and 1-inch
Wrenches, open-end, plumber's, and set of socket wrenches

Equipment	Boat Size			
	Less than 16 ft. Less than 4.8 m	16 ft.–26 ft. 4.8 m–7.9 m	26 ft.–40 ft. 7.9 m–12 m	40 ft.–65 ft. 12 m–20 m
Personal Flotation Devices (Life jackets)	One approved Type I, II III, or V wearable PFD for each person on board or being towed.	One approved Type I, II, III, or V device for each person on board or being towed on water skis, etc. In addition, one throwable Type IV device. Type V recreational hybrid PFDs, if carried exclusively, must be worn when the boat is underway. Other Type V PFDs must be approved for the activity for which the boat is being used.		
Visual Distress Signals	Approved visual distress signals for night use.	Must carry visual distress signals approved for use both at night and during the day.		
Fire Extinguishers (See note below)	At least one B-I approved portable fire extinguisher (not required on outboard motorboats less than 26 feet in length and not carrying passengers for hire, if the construction of such motorboats will not permit the entrapment of explosive or flammable gases or vapors, and if fuel tanks are not permanent.		At least two B-I approved fire extinguishers; OR at least one B-II approved portable fire extinguisher.	At least three B-I approved portable fire extinguishers; OR at least one B-I type, plus one B-II type approved portable fire extinguisher.
Bell and Whistle	Vessels less than 12 m (39.4 feet) in length must carry an efficient sound-making device.		All vessels of 12 m (39.4 feet) but less than 20 m (65.6 feet) in length must carry a whistle and a bell. The whistle must be audible for 0.5 nautical mile. The mouth of the bell must be at least 20 cm (7.87") in diameter.	
Ventilation: Boats built before August 1, 1980	At least two ventilator ducts fitted with cowls or their equivalent for the purpose of properly and efficiently ventilating the bilges of every closed engine and fuel-tank compartment of boats constructed or decked over after April 25, 1940, using gasoline as fuel or other fuels having a flashpoint of 110°F or less.			
Ventilation: Boats built on August 1, 1980 or later	At least two ventilator ducts for the purpose of efficiently ventilating every closed compartment that contains a gasoline engine and every closed compartment containing a gasoline tank, except those having permanently installed tanks that vent outside the boat and that contain no unprotected electrical devices. Engine compartments containing a gasoline engine with a cranking motor must contain power-operated exhaust blowers that can be controlled from the instrument panel.			
Backfire Flame Arrester	One approved device on each carburetor of all gasoline engines installed after April 25, 1940, with the exception of outboard motors.			

Note: A fixed extinguisher installed in a machinery space replaces one B-I portable fire extinguisher.

SAFETY

The legal safety requirements of federal and state authorities are a bare minimum. Here's what the American Sailing Association recommends small cruisers should carry in addition:

Ground tackle: Two anchors with no less than 200 feet (60 m) of rope or chain on each

Bailer or manual bilge pump

Flashlight and spare batteries

First-aid kit containing

First-aid manual	Antiseptic
Adhesive bandages in various sizes	Sunscreen
Three-inch (75-mm) sterile pads	Calamine lotion
Triangular bandages	Motion-sickness pills or patches
Rolled bandages, 1-inch (25-mm)	Tweezers and blunt scissors
Rolled bandages, 3-inch (75-mm)	Cotton balls or cotton wool
Aspirin or substitutes	Eyewash cup

Tool kit containing:

Screwdrivers, large and small

Phillips-head screwdriver

Wrench for every fastening on board

Sailmaker's needle, palm, and twine

Sail ties

Coil of nylon line

Assorted shackles, nuts, bolts, and screws

Vise-Grips

Hammer

Sharp knife and sharpening tool

High-quality duct tape

Lubricating spray

Hacksaw and several sharp blades

Navigation charts and equipment

Softwood plugs for through-hull fittings

Marine-band VHF radio transceiver

Safety harnesses for everyone on board

Lifebuoys—at least two, one near the helm

Buoyant heaving line

Tow rope

Foghorn

Steering and bearing compasses

Tables and Formulas

AVERAGE HUMAN SPACE REQUIREMENTS

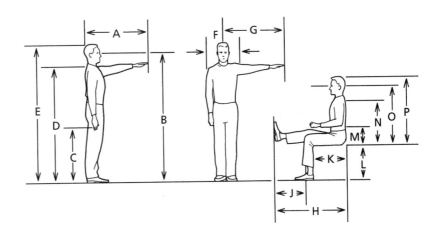

Key to Letters		Tall Man		Average Man		Small Woman	
		Inches	mm	Inches	mm	Inches	mm
A	Forward reach	36½	925	33¼	845	23½	600
B	Eye height	68¾	1,745	64	1,630	52¾	1,340
C	Hand height	33	840	29	740	25¾	655
D	Shoulder height	56½	1,435	55	1,400	47¼	1,200
E	Standing headroom	74	1,880	68½	1,740	57¼	1,455
F	Shoulder width	19¾	505	18¼	465	14¾	375
G	Side reach	36½	925	34¾	885	30	765
H	Back to bottom of foot	46½	1,185	41¾	1,060	35	890
J	Back to front of knee	26	660	23¼	590	20½	520
K	Thigh length	20½	520	18¾	480	16½	420
L	Sole to buttock	18½	470	16½	420	14¼	365
M	Elbow to buttock	10½	270	8½	220	5¾	145
N	Shoulder to buttock	25	640	22¾	580	18¾	480
O	Eye to buttock	33¼	845	28¾	730	24½	620
P	Sitting headroom	37¾	960	35½	900	29	740

BUNK DIMENSIONS FOR COMFORT

Note: One berth in four may safely be only 6 feet 1 inch (1.85 m) long.

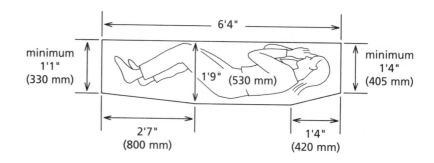

minimum
1'1"
(330 mm)

6'4"

minimum
1'4"
(405 mm)

1'9" (530 mm)

2'7"
(800 mm)

1'4"
(420 mm)

PLASTIC AND RUBBER FOAM FOR MATTRESSES AND CUSHIONS

Thickness	Comments
1 in. (25 mm)	Too thin for comfort on a hard base. Used for insulation on pipe berths with canvas bases.
2 in. (50 mm)	Not comfortable bedding on flat, hard base. Used for backrests and cockpit cushions.
3 in. (75 mm)	Bare minimum for bedding on hard base. Extensively used on very small boats and inexpensive production models.
4 in. (100 mm)	Comfortable on hard base. Standard on larger, quality craft.

EATING TABLE DIMENSIONS

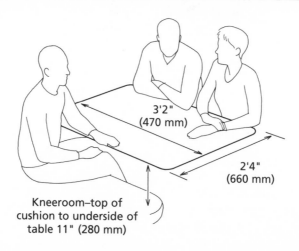

3'2"
(470 mm)

2'4"
(660 mm)

Kneeroom–top of
cushion to underside of
table 11" (280 mm)

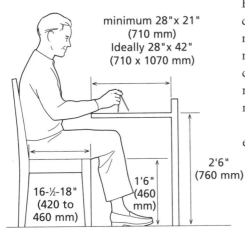

minimum 28"x 21"
(710 mm)
Ideally 28"x 42"
(710 x 1070 mm)

2'6"
(760 mm)

1'6"
(460
mm)

16-½-18"
(420 to
460 mm)

Even in the smallest of vessels, the minimum size for a chart table is 21 inches by 28 inches (530 mm by 710 mm). A table 22 inches by 36 inches (560 mm by 915 mm) will accept most charts folded once. Ideally, the chart table should measure 28 inches by 42 inches (530 mm by 1,100 mm), but few small yachts have that much space available.

About 100 charts, folded once, will fill a chart drawer to a depth of about 2 inches (50 mm).

METRIC PREFIXES

Names for units used in the metric system or SI (Système International) are formed by adding the following prefixes:

Prefix	Meaning	Symbol
Tera:	$\times$ 1,000,000,000,000	T
Giga:	$\times$ 1,000,000,000	G
Mega:	$\times$ 1,000,000	M
Kilo:	$\times$ 1,000	k
Hecto:	$\times$ 100	h
Deca:	$\times$ 10	da
Deci:	$\div$ 10	d
Centi:	$\div$ 100	c
Milli:	$\div$ 1,000	m
Micro:	$\div$ 1,000,000	μ
Nano:	$\div$ 1,000,000,000	n
Pico:	$\div$ 1,000,000,000,000	p

In addition, the prefix femto (f) denotes a factor of 10^{-15} and the prefix atto (a) denotes a factor of 10^{-18}.

Decimals of an Inch in Sixty-Fourths, and Millimeter Equivalents

Fraction	64ths	Decimal	Millimeters	Fraction	64ths	Decimal	Millimeters
	1	0.015625	0.397		33	0.515625	13.097
1/32	2	0.03125	0.794	17/32	34	0.53125	13.494
	3	0.046875	1.191		35	0.546875	13.891
1/16	4	0.0625	1.588	9/16	36	0.5625	14.288
	5	0.078125	1.984		37	0.578125	14.684
3/32	6	0.09375	2.381	19/32	38	0.59375	15.081
	7	0.109375	2.778		39	0.609375	15.478
1/8	8	0.125	3.175	5/8	40	0.625	15.875
	9	0.140625	3.572		41	0.640625	16.272
5/32	10	0.15625	3.969	21/32	42	0.65625	16.669
	11	0.171875	4.366		43	0.671875	17.066
3/16	12	0.1875	4.763	11/16	44	0.6875	17.463
	13	0.203125	5.159		45	0.703125	17.859
7/32	14	0.21875	5.556	23/32	46	0.71875	18.256
	15	0.234375	5.953		47	0.734375	18.653
1/4	16	0.250	6.350	3/4	48	0.750	19.050
	17	0.265625	6.747		49	0.765625	19.447
9/32	18	0.28125	7.144	25/32	50	0.78125	19.844
	19	0.296875	7.541		51	0.796875	20.241
5/16	20	0.3125	7.938	13/16	52	0.8125	20.638
	21	0.328125	8.334		53	0.828125	21.034
11/32	22	0.34375	8.731	27/32	54	0.84375	21.431
	23	0.359375	9.128		55	0.859375	21.828
3/8	24	0.375	9.525	7/8	56	0.875	22.225
	25	0.390625	9.922		57	0.890625	22.622
13/32	26	0.40625	10.319	29/32	58	0.90625	23.019
	27	0.421875	10.716		59	0.921875	23.416
7/16	28	0.4375	11.113	15/16	60	0.9375	23.813
	29	0.453125	11.509		61	0.953125	24.209
15/32	30	0.46875	11.906	31/32	62	0.96875	24.606
	31	0.484375	12.303		63	0.984375	25.003
1/2	32	0.500	12.700	1	64	1.000	25.400

DEFINITION OF DISPLACEMENT

Displacement is simply the total weight of a boat and everything aboard her as she floats in water. The terms *immersed hull volume, boat weight*, and *total displacement* are used interchangeably by designers. But displacement changes significantly with loading, so for practical reasons the displacement figure used for cruising boats by naval architects is the weight of a fully equipped vessel loaded and ready to go to sea. That weight includes all members of the crew, two-thirds of the provisions, and two-thirds of the fuel and water supplies.

DISPLACEMENT-TO-LENGTH (DL) RATIO

This simple ratio gives an idea of how "heavy" or "light" a boat is, without your being able to see her underwater body. The "tons" used here are long tons of 2,240 pounds, or metric tons of 1,000 kg, which almost equal long tons. For greater accuracy, multiply long tons by 1.016 to convert to metric tons.

DL ratio (U.S.) = tons displacement ÷ (waterline length in feet ÷ 100)³

OR

DL ratio (metric) = tons displacement ÷ (waterline length in meters ÷ 30.5)³

Example:

1. Boat displaces 12,500 pounds = 5.58 long tons.
2. Waterline length = 25 feet.
3. 5.58 ÷ (25 ÷ 100)³ = 5.58 ÷ (0.25 × 0.25 × 0.25).
4. 5.58 ÷ 0.015625 = 357.
5. Interpret the results in the table below, 357 = heavy displacement.

DL-ratio	Displacement
380:1 or greater	Very heavy
320:1 to 380:1	Heavy
250:1 to 320:1	Medium
120:1 to 250:1	Light
50:1 to 120:1	Very light
50:1 or less	Ultralight

CALCULATING THE SIZE OF A CRUISING BOAT

How big a boat do you need for long-distance cruising with reasonably comfortable living space and amenities? It depends on two factors: the number of crew and the weight of the stores.

To find the minimum required displacement of a cruising sailboat, within 10 percent, multiply the combined weight of crew and stores by 7.

Estimating Weight of Crew and Stores

For cruise-planning purposes, use these guidelines:

Crew: Multiply number of crew by 160 pounds (72 kg).

Stores: Allow 6 pounds (2.8 kg) per person per day.

Water: Allow 8.5 pounds (3.8 kg) per person per day.

Safety reserve: Multiply the total of stores and water by 1.5.

Personal gear: Allow 5 pounds (2.3 kg) per day, or a maximum of 120 pounds (55 kg) per person. For permanent liveaboards, a maximum of 500 to 1,000 pounds (225 to 450 kg) is more appropriate.

Example:

1. Find the minimum boat displacement needed for two people with water and provisions for 42 days.
2. Displacement (within 10 percent) = (weight of crew and stores) × 7.
3. Longest time between provisionings = 42 days.
4. Number of crew = 2. Crew weight = 2 × 160 = 320 pounds.
5. Daily stores = 6 pounds × 2 crew × 42 days = 504 pounds.
6. Water = 8.5 pounds × 2 crew × 42 days = 714 pounds.
7. Safety reserve = 504 (stores) + 714 (water) = 1,218 × 1.5 = 1,827.
8. Personal gear = 120 pounds × 2 = 240 pounds.
9. Total weight of stores, safety reserve, and personal gear = 1,827 + 240 = 2,067 pounds.
10. Displacement = 2,067 × 7 = 14,469 pounds or 6.5 tons.
11. Displacement within 10 percent = 13,000 pounds to 16,000 pounds (5.8 tons to 7 tons).

CALCULATING WATERPLANE AREA

Many useful calculations start with a boat's waterplane area. It's the area of a horizontal slice through the hull at water level.
This formula gives a close approximation:

Waterplane area = waterline length × waterline beam × 0.76.

Example:

1. Waterline length = 28 feet.
2. Waterline beam = 10 feet 6 inches.
3. Waterplane area = 28 × 10.5 × 0.76 = 223 square feet.

LOAD/IMMERSION FACTORS

To calculate how much of a load will put your boat an inch, or a centimeter, down on her marks, use this formula:

Pounds per inch immersion = waterplane area (square feet) × 5.34.

OR

Kilograms per centimeter immersion = waterplane area (square meters) × 10.25.

Example:

1. Boat's waterline length = 28 feet.
2. Waterline beam = 10 feet 10 inches.
3. Approximate waterplane area = 28 × 10.83 × 0.76 = 230.46 square feet.
4. Pounds per inch immersion = 230.46 × 5.34 = 1,231 pounds load per inch immersion.

SPEED OF DISPLACEMENT HULLS

The approximate maximum speed in knots of any displacement hull (one that does not plane) is governed by this formula:

Hull speed = $1.34 \times \sqrt{WL}$ (feet)

OR

Hull speed = $2.43 \times \sqrt{WL}$ (m)

A displacement boat with narrow beam will reach slightly higher speeds than indicated by this formula, but the speed of very beamy displacement boats will be slightly less than indicated.

KEEL AREA IN RELATION TO SAIL AREA

The size of a boat's centerboard or keel, in comparison with the amount of sail she carries, varies according to the underwater design. These rules of thumb indicate the percentage of lateral plane area compared with sail area:

Full-keel boats: Total lateral plane, including rudder, should be 12 to 16 percent of sail area.

Fin-keel boats: Area of fin keel (only) should be 7 to 10 percent of sail area.

Centerboard boats: Area of centerboard (only) may be as little as 5 percent of sail area.

RUDDERS

Balanced Rudder Proportions

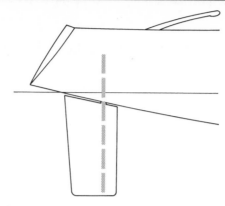

Rudder Area

For sailboats, rudder area should be 8 to 10 percent of the total lateral plane area.

Rudderstock Size

The size of a rudderstock depends on the area of the rudder, the speed of the boat, how the stock is supported, and the aspect ratio of the blade—the proportion of height to width.

These graphs appear in *The Nature of Boats,* by Dave Gerr (International Marine). They give recommended rudderstock sizes for solid bronze stocks. Solid stainless steel stocks may be about 10 percent less in diameter.

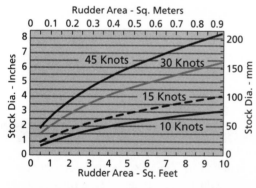

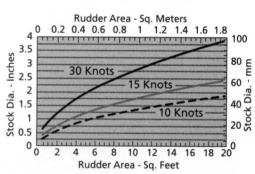

HUMAN POWER

The average man in good condition can produce about ¼ hp (0.2 kW) for about 40 minutes. He can produce between ⅐ and ⅙ hp (0.1 and 0.125 kW) for several hours at a time. This is sufficient to row a dinghy at a reasonable clip—say 3 to 4 knots—in calm water and no wind.

The maximum power from a highly trained male athlete for a burst of a few seconds is a little less than 2 hp (1.5 kW).

Conversion Factors

Note: Where a conversion factor in the following table is followed by "$\times 10^{-3}$" or by "$\times 10^{-4}$" and so forth, simply move the decimal point three or four places to the left, as appropriate.

Where a conversion factor is followed by "$\times 10^4$" or by "$\times 10^5$," shift the decimal point four or five places to the right.

Be aware that some metricated countries use a comma instead of a period to indicate the decimal point, and a blank space instead of a comma to indicate the thousands separator.

Example:

1. Convert 987 millimeters into feet.
2. Multiply 987 by conversion factor.
3. $987 \times 3.281 = 3{,}238.3$
4. Move the decimal point three places to the left = 3.2383 feet.

Example:

1. Convert 12.6 square yards into square millimeters.
2. Multiply 12.6 by conversion factor.
3. $12.6 \times 8.361 = 105.3486$.
4. Move the decimal point five places to the right = 10,534,860.0 square millimeters.

	To Convert	to	Multiply by
LENGTH	Inches	millimeters	25.40
	Feet	meters	0.3048
	Yards	meters	0.9144
	Nautical miles	kilometers	1.852
	Nautical miles	statute miles	1.1516
	Statute miles	nautical miles	0.8684
	Statute miles	kilometers	1.609
	Millimeters	inches	0.03937
	Millimeters	feet	3.281×10^{-3}
	Millimeters	meters	0.001
	Meters	kilometers	0.001
	Meters	statute miles	6.214×10^{-4}
	Meters	nautical miles	5.396×10^{-4}
	Meters	yards	1.094
	Meters	feet	3.281

To Convert	to	Multiply by
Kilometers	meters	1,000.0
Kilometers	statute miles	0.6214
Kilometers	nautical miles	0.5396

AREA

To Convert	to	Multiply by
Square inches	square feet	6.944×10^{-3}
Square inches	square millimeters	645.2
Square inches	square yards	7.716×10^{-4}
Square feet	square inches	144.0
Square feet	square yards	0.1111
Square feet	square millimeters	9.290×10^4
Square feet	square meters	0.09290
Square millimeters	square inches	1.550×10^{-3}
Square millimeters	square feet	1.076×10^{-5}
Square meters	square feet	10.76
Square meters	square yards	1.196
Square meters	square inches	1,550.0
Square kilometers	square miles	0.3861
Square yards	square meters	0.8361
Square yards	square feet	9.0
Square yards	square inches	1,296
Square yards	square millimeters	8.361×10^5
Square miles	square kilometers	2.590

VOLUME

To Convert	to	Multiply by
Cubic inches	cubic feet	5.787×10^{-4}
Cubic inches	cubic yards	2.143×10^{-5}
Cubic inches	milliliters	16.39
Cubic inches	liters	0.01639
Cubic feet	milliliters	28,320.0
Cubic feet	liters	28.32
Cubic feet	U.S. gallons	7.48052
Cubic feet	cubic inches	1,728.0
Cubic feet	cubic meters	0.02832
Cubic yards	Cubic feet	27.0
Cubic yards	Cubic inches	46,656.0
Cubic yards	Cubic meters	0.7646
Cubic yards	U.S. gallons	202.0
Cubic yards	liters	764.6
Fluid ounces	cubic inches	1.805
Fluid ounces	liters	0.02957
Imperial gallons	U.S. gallons	1.20095
U.S. gallons	imperial gallons	0.83267
U.S. gallons	cubic inches	231.0
U.S. gallons	cubic meters	3.785×10^{-3}
U.S. gallons	cubic yards	4.951×10^{-3}
U.S. gallons	liters	3.785
Cubic centimeters	milliliters	1.0

	To Convert	to	Multiply by
	Milliliters	cubic inches	0.06102
	Milliliters	cubic meters	10^{-6}
	Milliliters	cubic yards	1.308×10^{-6}
	Milliliters	U.S. gallons	2.642×10^{-4}
	Liters	cubic feet	0.03531
	Liters	cubic inches	61.02
	Liters	cubic meters	0.001
	Liters	cubic yards	1.308×10^{-3}
	Liters	U.S. gallons	0.2642
	Liters	U.S. pints	2.113
	Cubic meters	U.S. gallons	264.2
	Cubic meters	cubic feet	35.31
	Cubic meters	cubic yards	1.308
	Cubic meters	liters	1,000.0
WEIGHT	Ounces	grams	28.349527
	Ounces	pounds	0.0625
	Pounds	grams	453.5924
	Pounds	kilograms	0.4536
	Pounds	ounces	16.0
	Tons (long)	kilograms	1,016
	Tons (long)	pounds	2,240
	Tons (long)	tons (short)	1.120
	Tons (short)	ounces	29,166.66
	Tons (short)	pounds	2,000
	Tons (short)	tons (long)	0.89287
	Grams	kilograms	0.001
	Grams	milligrams	1,000
	Grams	pounds	2.205×10^{-3}
	Grams	ounces	0.03527
	Kilograms	pounds	2.205
	Kilograms	tons (long)	9.842×10^{-4}
	Kilograms	tons (short)	1.102×10^{-3}
SPEED	Miles/hour	kilometers/hour	1.609
	Miles/hour	feet/minute	88
	Miles/hour	feet/second	1.467
	Miles/hour	centimeters/second	44.70
	Miles/hour	knots	0.8684
	Feet/second	centimeters/second	30.48
	Feet/second	kilometers/hour	1.097
	Feet/second	knots	0.5921
	Feet/second	meters/minute	18.29
	Feet/second	miles/hour	0.6818
	Feet/second	miles/minute	0.01136

CONVERSION FACTORS

To Convert	to	Multiply by
Knots	feet/hour	6,076
Knots	kilometers/hour	1.8532
Knots	statute miles/hour	1.151
Knots	yards/hour	2,027
Knots	feet/second	1.689
Kilometers/hour	centimeters/second	27.78
Kilometers/hour	feet/minute	54.68
Kilometers/hour	feet/second	0.9113
Kilometers/hour	knots	0.5396
Kilometers/hour	meters/minute	16.67
Kilometers/hour	miles/hour	0.6214
Meters/second	feet/minute	196.8
Meters/second	feet/second	3.281
Meters/second	kilometers/hour	3.6
Meters/second	kilometers/minute	0.06
Meters/second	miles/hour	2.237
Meters/second	miles/minute	0.03728

DENSITY

Pounds/cubic foot	kilograms/cubic meter	16.02
Pounds/cubic foot	pounds/cubic inch	5.787×10^{-4}
Kilograms/cubic meter	pounds/cubic foot	0.06243
Kilograms/cubic meter	grams/cubic centimeter	0.001

ENERGY, STRESS, WORK

Kilograms/square meter	atmospheres	9.678×10^{-5}
Kilograms/square meter	pounds/square foot	0.2048
Kilograms/square meter	pounds/square inch	1.422×10^{-3}
Kilograms/square meter	tons/square inch	0.635
Pounds/square foot	kilograms/square meter	4.882
Pounds/square inch	kilograms/square meter	703.1
Tons/square inch	kilograms/square meter	1.575
Atmospheres	kilograms/square meter	10,332
Horsepower	kilowatts	0.7457
Horsepower	foot-pounds/minute	33,000
Horsepower	Btu/minute	42.44
Kilowatts	horsepower	1.341
Btu	kilowatt-hours	2.928×10^{-4}
Watts	Btu/minute	0.05688

TEMPERATURE

Degrees Centigrade	degrees Fahrenheit	$°F = °C \times \frac{9}{5} - 32$
Degrees Fahrenheit	degrees Centigrade	$°C = °F - 32 \times \frac{5}{9}$

Sources of Replacement Gear

Perhaps the most frustrating and time-consuming aspect of sailboat maintenance and repair is finding replacement parts. The work itself is often simple, and even pleasant if you have the right tools and the right parts. But finding the things you need, particularly for older boats, can be a major headache. Sailors are resourceful, and often get around this difficulty by coming up with new tricks to make old gear last another season or two, but inevitably there comes a time when only a new piece of gear will do.

What then? Start looking for a list of suppliers, of course. Unfortunately, some manufacturers pop out of the ground like mushrooms in spring, flourish briefly, and then disappear, leaving you with outdated source lists that add considerably to the frustration of refitting and repairing.

So you will find no highly perishable lists of sources for gear in this book. Instead, a different principle will be applied. It is this: If you spoonfeed a sailor with an up-to-date source list, he'll be happy for a week; if you teach him how to find things himself, he'll be happy for a lifetime.

Here, then, are some suggestions about where to start looking for that new plastic rubrail, that special lightbulb, or that very complicated zinc anode they stopped making 10 years ago.

Marine Stores Your local marine store is the obvious place to start looking. If they don't have the item in stock, ask if they can order it for you. Good marine stores keep catalogs from their major suppliers. Ask if you can browse through them. They're usually happy to share the catalogs if you are prepared to do all the searching. If there is no good marine store near you, order a free master catalog from one of the big mail-order marine supply companies, such as West Marine, 800-538-0775; M & E Marine, 800-541-6501; Defender Industries, 800-628-8225; or E & B Marine, 800-634-6382. Make sure you ask for the master catalog, not the skinny one they regularly send out to boatowners as a matter of course.

If you can't find what you're looking for in the master catalog, call their special orders department. The number's in the catalog. They'll call back within 24 hours to let you know if they've found a supplier. Members of BOAT/U.S. should call 800-568-0319 for that association's catalog.

Yacht Clubs In every yacht club there are some people who know everything about boats. If you have access to a club, make for the bar. Buy a member a drink. Ask if he or she knows where to find a replacement lower-shroud wobble remover for a 1973 Frantic sloop. Pretty soon the whole place will be abuzz. Take a notebook, because you're going to get a lot of different answers, all of them guaranteed correct. One might be helpful.

If no member can help you, ask if you can leave a plea for information on their bulletin board.

Class Associations
If you own a one-design club racer, there's a good chance that other owners have formed a class association somewhere. And you can be sure they have already found a source of supply for the spare part you need.

Yacht clubs often keep lists of class associations. You can also try your area sail-racing association; the yacht club ought to have the address handy. Otherwise you can try The United States Sailing Association at P.O. Box 209, 2nd Floor, Goat Island Marine Building, Newport, RI 02840; 401-849-5200. Or try the latest annual issue of *The Sailor's Sourcebook*, (The Sailing Company), 401-847-1588.

Watch for regattas offering racing for your class of boat. Someone there is bound to have the answer you seek.

The Builder
If it's still in business, the company that built your boat will be a good source of information about replacement gear. If you're lucky, you won't have to look any further. Otherwise, they may be able to point you to the original equipment manufacturer or suggest an alternative source.

The Designer
The font of all knowledge about your boat is the designer. Most designers are pleased to hear from owners, particularly owners who are clever enough to keep the conversation short and throw in a little praise. All designers keep extensive libraries of gear catalogs, and most will promise to look up the answer if they don't know it offhand. You skill in flattery will be reflected in the speed with which your call is returned.

Engine Manufacturers and Marine Mechanics
If you need a part for an engine and the manufacturer is still in business, start right there. Ask for the parts department, and if they just fall about laughing when you ask for a head gasket for a 1938 single-cylinder Thrashabout Model-A, try the public relations department. Even if they're no more helpful, they're trained to be polite.

Marine mechanics are a fertile source of information about spare parts, and will often be able to tell you who can fabricate the part you need if nobody makes it anymore. Of course, they are usually more forthcoming if they believe you might hire them to work on your engine.

Boatyards
Boatyards, too, are more likely to tell you where to find parts if they think they'll get the work of fitting them. Some, quite understandably, are loath to part with information about their sources, and will give you a gentle brush-off if your boat isn't in their yard. But there's no harm in asking around and trying your luck. Others may be more generous with their source lists.

Dockmasters and Harbormasters Just about everybody in the pleasureboat business brushes up against a dock master or a harbormaster occasionally. Consequently, harbormasters are a good source of tips about where to find marine gear. The trick is to catch them when they're not busy, when they have a couple of minutes to talk to you. If you're lucky, you might manage this by phone. Success is more likely, though, if you hang around in person and seize the right opportunity.

Failing all else, ask if you can leave a notice on the harbormaster's bulletin board. It's seen by everyone in the marina sooner or later.

Annual Sourcebooks Two comprehensive directories of the complete U.S. sailboat industry are published annually.

The Sailor's Sourcebook for 1996 was 244 pages long and featured up-to-date lists and illustrations of sailboats, designers, hardware, rigging, electronics, sailing schools, charter companies, safety gear, and custom builders. It also carried advertisements and included product indexes.

To order a copy, call The Sailing Company (*Sailing World* and *Cruising World* magazines) at 401-847-1588, or write to P.O. Box 3400, Newport, RI 02840-0992. The 1996 issue sold for $4.95.

The annual Sailboat Buyers Guide, a complete guide to boats and gear, was 408 pages long in 1996, and also provided extensive lists of gear and services touching every aspect of the sailboat business in the United States, including a sailing industry directory. It's published by *SAIL* magazine, and the 1996 issue sold for $8.95, including postage and handling. To order a copy, call 800-362-8433 or 617-630-3721.

Cruisers' Radio Nets If you're a liveaboard cruiser, your source list is as near as your radio. In most ports, cruisers have organized communication networks on VHF radio. Find out when and where the local net broadcasts, and ask your fellow cruisers for help in tracing the parts you need. Often, a land-based net controller has close contacts with a marine supply store, so if your cruising friends can't help, the controller will likely be able to make a suggestion.

The Internet Those of you with PCs or laptops on board can ask for help from boaters all over the world. If you have access to a boating home page or bulletin board, there will be plenty of Net surfers eager to discuss your problem to death. On the Internet, someone, somewhere always knows something. It's worth trying. And if you don't have access to the Net, you probably have a friend with a computer who sits up late at night and wouldn't mind becoming a little more hollow-eyed on your account.

Letters to the Editor Some public-spirited boating newspapers and magazines accept letters to the editor asking for help in tracing replacement parts. There is no charge for this service, but you should keep your letter very brief, certainly under 100 words.

Send copies of the same letter to all the marine publications in your area. Some may use it, others certainly won't, but you have nothing to lose. If you make your letter appealing, informative, or entertaining in some way, it's more likely to be used.

Advertisements

If you're really desperate, you can pay for an ad in the classified section of a boating publication. Always give a phone number or an e-mail address for replies.

Boaters' Directories

Several publishing firms produce free local boating directories with white pages and yellow pages listing suppliers of gear and services in your area. You'll find these directories at marine stores, yacht clubs, marina offices, yacht brokers' offices, and outlets for sailing publications. Most are published annually, so the information will be fairly up to date.

Marine Trade Associations

Almost any place that has a significant population of pleasure boats will also have a marine trade association. Its primary function is to further the wealth and well-being of its members, of course, but in the interests of better customer relations these associations will often help you track down the supplier you need. Your nearest library will help you get the name and number of your local marine trade association if it isn't listed in the Yellow Pages of your phone book.

The National Marine Manufacturers Association, with about 1,500 members, is located at 401 N. Michigan Avenue, Chicago, IL 60611, and the phone number is 312-836-4747.

Another national trade association is the Marine Retailers Association of America, 155 N. Michigan Avenue, Suite 5230, Chicago, IL 60611; 312-938-0359.

Sailing Magazines

Apart from sending letters to the editor and placing ads, you can call the editorial staff of your favorite sailing magazine for help. Unless it's a really small publication, you're not likely to be put through to the editor, though. You'll almost certainly be diverted to an editorial assistant, though you can try to avoid this by asking to speak to the technical writer whose name should be given in the staff box of each magazine. Some magazines care more about reader relations than others, and you'll be able to judge what kind of magazine it is by the reception you get and the speed of the follow-up to your query. You may want to revise your subscription list after a couple of calls.

If you subscribe to *Practical Sailor*, the consumer magazine that accepts no trade advertising, you're entitled to call them with queries at 401-849-7432 from 11.30 A.M. to 1 P.M. (Eastern) on Tuesdays and Thursdays. The address is 75 Holly Hill Lane, Greenwich, CT 06836.

Here are addresses and phone numbers for other major sailing magazines in the United States.

Cruising World, P.O. Box 3400, Newport, RI 02840; 401-847-1588.

Heartland Boating, P.O. Box 1067, Martin, TN 38237; 901-587-6791.

Lakeland Boating, 1560 Sherman Avenue, Suite 1220, Evanston, IL 60201; 708-869-5400.

Latitude 38, P.O. Box 1678, Sausalito, CA 94966; 415-383-8200.

Motor Boating & Sailing, 250 W. 55th Street, New York, NY 10019; 212-489-9258.

Offshore, 220-9 Reservoir Street, Needham, MA 02194; 617-449-6204.

SAIL, 275 Washington Street, Newton, MA 02158; 617-964-8948.

Sailing magazine, 125 E. Main Street, Port Washington, WI 53074; 414-284-3494.

Sailing World, 5 John Clarke Road, Newport, RI 02840; 401-847-1588.

WoodenBoat, P.O. Box 78, Brooklin, ME 04616; 207-359-4651.

Yachting, 5th Floor, 2 Park Avenue, New York, NY 10016; 212-779-5300.

Boat Shows   Major boat shows are wonderful sources of information about gear and supplies for repair and maintenance. Take a notebook, and be sure to do your homework in the nuts-and-bolts section before you become enchanted by the shiny new boats and their dazzling new electronics.

Libraries   Your local library will have a reference librarian whose unenviable job it is to deal with strange queries from the public all day long. On the whole, reference librarians are a gracious lot who suffer fools gladly. Savvier fools know that subtle praise can bear extraordinary results.

Boating Organizations

American Boat and Yacht Council

Develops and publishes safe standards for designing, building, equipping, and maintaining yachts and commercial vessels. Also publishes *Boating Information, a Bibliography and Source List*, detailing over 1,300 books, pamphlets, articles, and videos related to pleasure boating.
Address: 3069 Solomon's Island Road, Edgewater, MD 21037
Telephone: 410-956-1050

The comprehensive manual of safe standards (it weighs seven pounds) costs $125 but is available only to members. Membership is open to all at $125 a year.

American Boat Builders and Repairers Assoc.

A nationwide trade association committed to improving methods of repair and maintenance in the boating industry. Also adjudicates disputes between owners and boatyards, marinas, and manufacturers.
Address: 715 Boylston Street, Boston, MA 02116
Telephone: 617-266-6800

Boat Owners Assoc. of the United States

A national organization that conveys the views of boaters to Congress and federal agencies. Operates a consumer protection bureau and adjudicates disputes between boatowners and marine professionals. Publishes the news journal *BOAT/U.S. Reports*.
Address: 880 S. Pickett Street, Alexandria, VA 22304
Telephone: 703-823-9550

BOAT/U.S. Foundation

Distributes free safety literature and promotes boating education. This non-profit organization runs a toll-free CourseLine detailing free boating courses: 800-336-BOAT. Maintains records of boating accidents and safety issues. Produces a useful *Boater's Source Directory* with a grant from the U.S. Coast Guard.
Address: 880 S. Pickett Street, Alexandria, VA 22304
Telephone: 703-823-9550

Canadian Coast Guard

Responsible for enforcing boating rules and regulations in Canada. Broadcasts weather reports and warnings to mariners. Operates search-and-rescue vessels and aircraft. Educates pleasure boaters and publishes safety material.
Address: Canada Building, Minto Place, 344 Slater Street, Ottawa, ON, K1A ON7, Canada
Telephone: 613-991-3119

For publications or free information on boating courses, call 613-990-3116.

Defense Mapping Agency (DMA)	This U.S. agency publishes charts of foreign waters as well as navigation reference works such as the *American Practical Navigator*, written by Nathaniel Bowditch in 1799. The agency also publishes lists of radio aids, and the international code of signals.
	Address: Office of Distribution Services, Code: IMA, 6500 Brookes Lane, Washington, DC 20315
	Telephone: 202-227-3048

Federal Communications Commission (FCC)	Issues marine operator and station licenses. Prescribes regulations for radio communications, and qualifications for operators.
	Address: Aviation and Marine Division, 2025 M Street NW, Washington, DC 20554
	Telephone: 202-632-7197
	For VHF Marine Radio License applications, call the FCC's Gettysburg office to locate your nearest FCC field office.
	Telephone: 717-337-1212

Marine Retailers Assoc. of America	A national trade association guarding the interests of retail outlets selling pleasure boats and marine equipment. A potential source of information about hard-to-find parts and gear.
	Address: 155 N. Michigan Avenue, Suite 5230, Chicago, IL 60611
	Telephone: 312-938-0359

National Marine Manufacturers Association	A major trade association representing manufacturers of boats, motors, and all kinds of boating equipment. Puts forward its members' views to Congress and industrial bodies. Sponsors national boat shows. Another potential source of information about parts and gear.
	Address: 401 N. Michigan Avenue, Chicago, IL 60611
	Telephone: 312-836-4747

National Ocean Access Project	See listing "Resources for Disabled Sailors."

National Ocean Service (NOS)	This agency of the National Oceanographic and Atmospheric Administration (NOAA) surveys the coast of the United States and its island territories, and publishes charts, tide tables, and chart catalogs.
	Address for publication and chart orders: Distribution Division, National Ocean Service, 6501 Lafayette Avenue, Riverdale, MD 20737-1199
	Telephone number for credit-card orders: 301-436-6990

ORGANIZATIONS

National Sailing Industry Assoc. A trade association comprising charter companies, boat manufacturers, hardware manufacturers, and sailing schools. Sponsors the free Learn to Sail Hotline, 800-447-4700, and publishes information about community sailing programs.
Address: 401 N. Michigan Avenue, Chicago, IL 60611
Telephone: 312-836-4747

Resources for Disabled Sailors These two nonprofit groups provide opportunities for people with disabilities to learn to sail, and they promote similar activities nationwide:
National Ocean Access Project, P.O. Box 657, Newport, RI 02840 *Telephone:* 401-849-9090

Shake-A-Leg, P.O. Box 1002, Newport, RI 02840 *Telephone:* 401-849-8898

Shake-A-Leg Miami, 2600 S. Bayshore Drive, Miami, FL 33133 *Telephone:* 305-858-5550

A slide/cassette program and a 114-page book (also available in Braille) *Boating for the Handicapped: Guidelines for the Physically Disabled*, are available from the National Center on Employment of the Handicapped, Human Resources Center, Albertson, NY 11507 *Telephone:* 516-747-5400

Shake-A-Leg See listing "Resources for Disabled Sailors."

Underwriters Laboratories, Inc. An independent, nonprofit organization conducting tests for public safety. Develops marine safety standards and tests marine products. Publishes *Standards for Safety for Recreational Boats* and a directory of marine products.
Address for publication orders: Underwriters Laboratories, Inc., Publications Stock, 333 Pfingsten Road, Northbrook, IL 60062
Telephone: 919-549-1565

U.S. Coast Guard Conducts search-and-rescue missions, installs and maintains aids to navigation, and enforces laws relating to safety, drugs, and marine sanitation devices. Operates a free Boating Safety Hotline, 800-368-5647, and publishes *Federal Requirements for Recreational Boats.*
Address: The Commandant (G-NAB), Boating Safety Department, U.S. Coast Guard, 2100 Second Street SW, Washington, DC 20593-0001
Telephone: 202-267-0972

United States Sailing Assoc. (U.S. Sailing) The U.S. national authority for sailboat racing and the sport of sailing. Promotes sailing and sail training through the voluntary efforts of clubs and individuals at all levels. Liaises with other national, international, and Olympic bodies. Publishes the monthly magazine *American Sailor* and the International Yacht Racing Rules.
Address: P.O. Box 209, 2nd Floor, Goat Island Marine Building, Newport, RI 02840
Telephone: 401-849-5200

Index

To my mother,
Catherine Christiana Vigor

When John Vigor emigrated from England to South Africa at the age of 13, he developed a passion for sailing that has never let up.

He has since raced and cruised on dozens of boats ranging in size from 11 feet to 72 feet, winning a national championship in the International Mirror class and putting in 15,000 miles of ocean voyaging.

As a journalist, he worked for major metropolitan daily newspapers in Britain, South Africa, and the United States. He wrote a popular humor column six days a week for nearly 20 years for the largest daily newspaper in Durban, South Africa, and has contributed sailing articles to *Cruising World, SAIL, Practical Boat Owner, Yachting Monthly* and other major sailing magazines.

In 1987, he sailed his 31-foot sloop from Durban to the United States with his American wife, June, and their 17-year-old son, Kevin. He joined the board of *The San Diego Union-Tribune* as an editorial writer, and later became managing editor of *Sea* magazine in Newport Beach, California.

He's the author of *Danger, Dolphins, and Ginger Beer* (Atheneum), a sailing adventure novel for 8 to 12 year-olds—also published in Germany as *Segelsommer mit Delphinen* (Carlsen)—and *The Practical Mariner's Book of Knowledge* (International Marine), a fascinating collection of 420 nautical rules of thumb.

He now lives in Oak Harbor, Washington, where he writes and edits books about sailing when he's not exploring Puget Sound and the San Juan Islands in his refurbished, 28-year old Santana 22, *Tagati*.

Published by International Marine

10 9 8 7 6 5 4 3 2 1

Copyright © 1997 John Vigor
All rights reserved. The publisher takes no responsibility for the use of any of the materials or methods described in this book, nor for the products thereof. The name "International Marine" and the International Marine logo are trademarks of The McGraw-Hill Companies.

The author and publisher have made every effort to ensure the accuracy of the facts and figures in this book. No guarantee is given or implied that the information in this book is accurate, and the responsibility for any consequences arising from the use of these data lies solely with the reader.

Questions regarding the content of this book should be addressed to:
International Marine
P.O. Box 220
Camden, ME 04843
Questions regarding the ordering of this book should be addressed to:
The McGraw-Hill Companies
Customer Service Department
P.O. Box 547
Blacklick, OH 43004
Retail customers: 1-800-262-4729;
Bookstores: 1-800-233-4726

The Sailor's Assistant is printed on 60-pound Renew Opaque Vellum, an acid-free paper that contains 50 percent recycled waste paper (preconsumer) and 10 percent postconsumer waste paper.
Printed by R.R. Donnelley
Design by Cia Boynton
Production by Cia Boynton, Mary Ann Hensel, Molly Mulhern

Unless otherwise noted, all illustrations by Jim Sollers
Edited by Jonathan Eaton, Tom McCarthy, Ellen Egan
Technical assistance by Eric Sponberg, Bill Brogdon, David Seidman

Library of Congress Cataloging-in-Publication Data
Vigor, John.
The sailor's assistant : reference data for maintenance, repair, and cruising / John Vigor
p. cm. — (The International Marine sailboat library)
Includes index.
ISBN 0-07-067476-0
1. Sailboats Maintenance and repair Handbooks, manuals, etc.
2. Seamanship—Handbooks, manuals, etc. I. Title. II. Series.
VM351.V52 1996
623.88'223—dc20   96-5719
CIP